Mick Byrne
Alice Taylor
Sr Hele
Bishop C
Archbishop Walton
Eileen Reid
Joseph O'Connor
Jimmy Magee
Jack Charlton
Gordon Wilson

I believe

Based on the RTÉ radio series of the same name

VERITAS

First published 2001 by
Veritas Publications
7/8 Lower Abbey Street
Dublin I
Ireland

Email publications@veritas.ie
Website www.veritas.ie

ISBN I 85390 598 4

A catalogue record for this book is available from the British Library.

Cover design by Bill Bolger
Printed in the Republic of Ireland by Betaprint Ltd, Dublin

Veritas books are printed on paper made from the wood pulp of managed forests.
For every tree felled, at least one tree is planted, thereby renewing natural
resources.

Dedication

To my good friend Brian Carthy,
who reminds me constantly of the wisdom of George Bernard
Shaw's advice not to 'waste time on people who don't know
what they think', in gratitude for past kindnesses.

Acknowledgments

The book is based on the radio series *I Believe,* which was transmitted on RTÉ in 2001.

I am particularly grateful to Ann Marie O'Callaghan who initially commissioned the *I Believe* series for RTÉ Radio 1 and to Helen Shaw for her generous support for this book and my other radio projects.

I would like to express my thanks to all the people who gave interviews and allowed me to profile them in this book.

I am grateful to my good friend Fr Dan O'Connor for his friendship and many kindnesses down through the years.

Some of these pieces appeared originally in *Reality* magazine. I am very grateful to Gerry Moloney, editor of *Reality,* for permission to reprint them.

I would also like to record my appreciation for my good friend, Don Mullan, for his practical help and support.

I am indebted to Maura Hyland, Helen Carr, Toner Quinn and all at Veritas for their help and encouragement.

CONTENTS

INTRODUCTION

Hello darkness my old friend
I've come to talk with you again.
(Simon and Garfunkel)

Belief. So easy to take for granted. Then, just when you least expect it, something happens to shatter it to its foundations.

My mother's voice was fractured with emotion as she spoke down the crackling line. Although her voice was scarcely audible her words are forever imprinted in my memory: 'Prepare yourself for an awful shock. Are you sitting down?' The blackest possible scenarios exploded through my brain. Except that one. 'Poor Oliver got a heart-attack this morning and died in Bertie's shed. The ambulance came and took him away. Can you come home?'

The foundations I thought were firm under my feet crumbled. Oliver was my best friend. My next door neighbour. My cousin. My soulmate. I've been told that from a certain angle we could have been mistaken for twins. He was the brother I never had.

My aunt Sheila met me at the train station in Athlone. We just nodded to each other. The first three miles passed in silence. Finally she broke the ice: 'He never looked better. He looks the cut of you. Ye have the same forehead.' Her words were like a dagger to my heart. My composure started to crumble but I fought against it. Heaven knows why I bothered.

'What size was he?' she asked. The finality of his death hit home with brutal force. From then on I would have to think of him in the past tense. 'Six foot seven and three quarters,' I mumbled. She continued: 'They couldn't find a coffin big enough for him. They had to have him propped up in the first coffin and send for a second one to Castlebar. It didn't arrive until two or three this morning.' Another crisis would develop when they tried to remove him from the wake house. They had to take down three doors to remove his remains. I thought back to my sister's wedding where his giant frame caused a lot of problems as he danced 'The Siege of Ennis'.

At last we arrived at our destination. I braced myself for the saddest moment of my life. It was a weird experience to walk through the door. I wanted to turn back, but something inside me kept me walking on. I hadn't expected to see his body in the living room. I had tried to prepare myself for this moment. But when the stark reality of his corpse was just feet away from me it was frightening in the extreme. I went to offer words of consolation to his family – but it was they who comforted me.

My mind was spinning with questions. Oliver was just thirty-three years of age. I could not comprehend why his radiant eyes had to surrender their sight. Nor why his articulate voice had to give away its speech. Justice should not allow the sacrifice of such innocent wealth.

It was only then that I realised his hands were so massive. Like a badly faded photocopy, a fragment of conversation I had with my mother over twenty years earlier returned to me: when he was a boy the doctor told him that his hands were too big for the rest of his body. At the time I thought he was talking nonsense. Now I think I know what he meant.

They were joined together in a prayerful position around his rosary beads. To be honest, they scared the hell out of me. They were snow white. It was as if all the blood had been drained out of them. My mind raced back to the last time I saw him alive when he walked into our kitchen with all the energy of a hurricane.

For the first time I noticed that an awful lot of people call him Ollie. Never once did I call him by that name. Well-meaning sympathisers trotted out soothing phrases: 'It's God's holy will.' Right then, I wished God had never been invented.

Another said: 'It's happy for him. There's something beautiful about a young death.' Happy? Beautiful? I wanted to scream at such a perversion of language. But it was not the time nor the place. Even if I had the energy.

My eyes met his mother's. The fellowship of the besieged was firmly established. I knew instinctively that all that was keeping her going was the thought of joining Oliver in a higher, more perfect world.

Oliver and I talked for thousands of hours and yet so many important things between us were left unsaid. What is it about us men that makes us so reticent about talking about our emotions? So many of us live in curious relationships – based on closeness and distance. There is often a very deep bond between us but we rarely or never openly or publicly express our feelings for each other. Is it not time we finally moved from emotional adolescence to maturity? I am not sure why, but I felt compelled to touch his forehead. The coldness of death repelled me and I pulled back my hand immediately.

For the first time, I discovered that tears taste of salt. His sister, Mary-Teresa, offered me a tissue and I knew that for her too the pain was almost unbearable.

As the crowd gathered, Oliver's many qualities were analysed. He was a very astute judge of people. Seldom did he rush into judgment. Rarely, if ever, did he judge by appearances. He always probed beneath the surface. He had the happy knack of dissecting what people said with the precision of a surgeon's knife. Although he was not a great television fan he watched the news religiously. God, I wished I could buy back just another ten minutes with him. Memories scampered through the mists of the past. As a boy, Oliver

had a brush with mortality when he was struck down by a severe
bout of pneumonia. I remember my mother coming home and
saying it was very doubtful if he would make it through the
weekend. That night we offered up the rosary for him. For once, I
didn't spend the time making designs on the wallpaper with my
finger, but gave the Godline my all. Then I wrote a letter to *Hospitals
Request* asking them to play a request for Oliver – even though he was
not in hospital. My mother always credited his recovery to the fact
that his family had the only phone in the village. They could get the
doctor quicker than anybody else. If I heard that story once I heard
it a thousand times.

Driving to the funeral parlour that evening, a white cat raced
across the road in front of me. I braked hard and the only damage
was to my blood pressure. The cat had nine lives. Oliver got only one.

I met a sea of familiar and half-forgotten faces. Some of them I
hadn't seen since his father's funeral twenty-two years ago that
month. Father Time had not been kind to all of them, and I had the
persistent embarrassment of not knowing the right names. A few,
like his cousin, Joe Donnelly, I recognised just by their voices.
'You've grown an awful lot,' was the most common verdict on me.

The last time I saw Oliver alive he joked and laughed and was full
of the joys of life. Now, although he looked splendid in the new grey
suit he only wore three times, it still unnerved me to see him there.

For three hours the crowds filed past his coffin. But time didn't
matter, for then it didn't exist.

A good sprinkling of politicians were in attendance. 'Is it for me,
or because there is an election a few months away?', Oliver would
have asked. One of their number strode up to the coffin with an air
of purpose. To date, his biggest political achievement had been his
own advancement. The man paused before me and knitted his brow,
as though puzzled, before finding his second breath. His mouth
opened like a landed fish and when he eventually spoke the words
had no impact. He offered me his sincere sympathy, but his roaming

eyes said otherwise. I could sense Oliver whispering: 'Does he think we're fools?'

On the third day Oliver was buried. His funeral was a very moving occasion. The grief, though intensely personal, was generously shared. The local community responded magnificently, as they always did in times of adversity. Everyone rallied around. Every seat in the house was crammed with relatives and neighbours, all with mournful faces. They had good reason to mourn in this court of human suffering. Minutes before the ceremony began there was an explosion of noise. Every head in the chapel turned to see business colleagues of Oliver's brothers emerge from a helicopter. There's never been anything like it seen in Curraghboy Church. This was mega – maybe mega, mega. Two neighbours shook their heads at each other ruefully. One said sadly to the other: 'You nor I will never get a send-off like this.' The strains of the organ instantly recaptured the solemnity of the occasion.

Oliver's brother Tommy did the reading. Later I heard someone describe him as 'a horse of a man'. Down here, that's a great compliment.

Oliver's sister, Martina, had asked me to read the communion reflection. I was at once honoured and petrified. The reflection was written on a page from a child's copy. It is now folded neatly in the old, battered box that I call my treasure chest – home to my most precious mementos.

The next hour or so is a complete haze: it's as if I've lost a piece of my life. The graveyard is on the top of an exposed hill. 'This must be the cauldest spot in Ireland,' a stranger said to me. A few drops of rain fell. I suspected they were tears of anger for a deed wrong and absurd. Oliver's coffin was laid into the ground and then draped in a blanket of hay. 'The finest of stuff,' he would have said.

He was laid to rest in an austere ceremony. Tradition in the locality dictates that the nearest neighbours, on the prompting of the bereaved, dig the grave and fill the clay over the coffin with a sense of privilege and decorum. The frozen clay seemed to resent the willing shovels. There was a finality about the proceedings in the tap-tap-tap as the back of the spade shaped the remaining mound of fresh clay. What really crucified me, though, was the sound of clods of earth crashing on the coffin. Now we will be forever friends in two different worlds.

As the final shovelfuls of clay were thrown on the grave, the sun came out of hiding like a scene from an autumnal coloured photograph. The symbol surely was the reality; Oliver had risen with the Son.

I waited until the mourners had departed to be alone with him for a final moment. I prayed to buy him some shares in the hereafter. Now I now why 'goodbye' is the most painful word in the English language. Parting is no sweet sorrow.

My grandfather – my surrogate father after my real daddy died when I was only five – is buried almost beside Oliver. Unlike Oliver, the swirling tide of death had liberated him from the nightmare of a lengthy illness. He is the ghost I carry around within me. It comforted me to think that the two most important men ever in my life lay almost side-by-side. For a moment, I longed to be with both of them – but my time had not yet come.

The morning after my darkest day. I had found it hard to sleep the previous night. There was nothing I could do to keep my eyes closed. The images of Oliver under six feet of clay were as clear as a mirror's reflection. When I finally fell asleep, I dreamt of a giant spider. I had never seen such a disturbing image. There was haunting music all around. The spider was singing. Its song was the web of death. I pleaded with the spider to spare Oliver, but he just laughed at me as he cast his shadow still wider.

Now coming home will always be a sad occasion for me. The time came to return to the world of work. I called in to say goodbye to Oliver's family. How could someplace so familiar become so alien? His ghost whispered from every corner. Every piece of furniture had its unique memory of him. I discussed incidents and accidents with his mother. When it was time for me to go neither of us could find the words to convey our feelings. But really there was no need just then.

I returned to my Rathmines flat. The milk had gone sour. The bread was turning a sickly bluish-green. It was hard to believe it was only five days since I was there last. I felt I'd aged ten years. I sat staring at the television for hours — even though I hadn't the set switched on. In this state the sands of time shift slowly. A strange paralysis invaded me.

What did I believe now? Could I believe anything? Over the next few months the question of belief continued to niggle at the back of my mind. I started to become fascinated not by belief in the abstract but by what other people believed. A very simple idea for a radio series was born. Why not just ask people what they believed?

The series was broadcast on RTÉ Radio One between January and April 2001. At the time, I had never thought about turning it into a book, but a phone call from Toner Quinn in Veritas changed all that. The following nineteen profiles are, in the broadest sense, testimonies of personal belief. They include people I interviewed, not just for the *I Believe* series, but some of the many people I've interviewed down through the years.

There is no attempt made to link the profiles. They are included because they were, in their very different ways, people who impressed me.

TO GOD THROUGH THE FIELDS
Alice Taylor

In 1988 the world of Irish publishing was rocked by the runaway success of a book from an unlikely candidate for superstardom. Alice Taylor was born on a farm near Newmarket in County Cork. She worked as a telephonist in Killarney and Bandon until she married, when she moved to Innishannon. She ran a guesthouse at first, then the supermarket and post office. She and her husband, Gabriel Murphy, have four sons and one daughter.

To School Through the Fields, her first book of memoirs of country life, quickly became one of the biggest selling books ever published in Ireland. Her sequels, *Quench the Lamp*, *The Village*, *Country Days* and *The Night Before Christmas*, also captured the pulse and sinews of rural Ireland and topped the best-seller charts.

In recent years, she has switched from chronicling the fading world of village life to writing fiction. In 1997 her first novel, *The Woman of the House*, was a critical and commercial success. She has also published a sequel, *Across the River*.

Catholicism cast a long shadow over all aspects of Irish society in Alice's childhood. There was a heavy wooden crucifix nailed up on a wall in most homes, flanked by pictures of sickly-yellow and gloomy apostles. More saints and wounded martyrs watched over other rooms. Reading material consisted largely of religious magazines like the *Sacred Heart*, the *Far East* and the *Messenger*, though amongst the farming community the *Farmer's Journal* was their Bible.

After a few moments in Alice Taylor's company the years roll back. There was the obligatory excursion for confession for which people queued interminably. On the window-ledges, huge, white candles flickered slightly as a draught touched them, then shone as brightly as before.

Alice's happiest memories from her Catholic childhood are those when she was engaged on a sensual level. She had a particular reverence for Benediction. She loved the choir's singing, the air warm and heavy with incense and bodies, and the tinkling of a bell. There always seemed to be a chorus of stifled coughing coming from the pews from nervous parishioners, answering awkwardly to the priest's promptings. In silence and solemnity the priest climbed towards the tabernacle. The monstrance glittering like a metallic sun as it moved into the shape of a cross before a mass of adoring eyes. Against the solemn backdrop of the mass, the smell of incense was more beautiful than a springtime primrose.

'I suppose, in the Ireland I grew up in, religion was a very strong influence. We had a sacred heart lamp in our kitchen and we changed the flowers regularly. I'm not sure what it instilled in us, but it was part of our background.

'My mother rounded us all up to say the rosary and I can remember arguments going on and kicks under the chair as the rosary was going on and I can remember looking out the window and watching the cows and counting them as a way of counting the rosary so I'm not sure there was much piety involved there!

'My mother was a very traditional Catholic. My father had a totally different approach. His God could be found out in the fields and was seen as part of nature. I always appreciated the God of the fields and the God of nature. It was just part of us. My father would set us down when we'd have breakfast on Sunday morning and he'd turn on the radio and we'd listen to religious services on the BBC which was kind of unusual and he'd always say, "Listen to what's going on now because you'll be hearing the exact same in our own church." He always felt that no one person nor group had a right to take hold of God.'

Like her father, Alice found it easy to find God in nature.

'One thing that really takes hold of my mind is the rogation days. I think it was the three days before the Ascension. My father and the other men would go out in the evening and bless the crops. I loved the sense that there was nobody there between them and their own land and God, as they asked God to bless their work. It was a lovely custom and brought God very close to them in the fields. This year I went out into my own garden and blessed it with Holy Water on rogation day. I realised then that when you grow up, you do absorb it, even though you may not be conscious of it at the time. It colours your life afterwards.

'My grandmother was quite a strict woman and she lived near us. In bed at night, she taught me a verse of this long, long prayer to my guardian angel and we learned a verse at night. This is the nicest, warmest memory of my grandmother because she was very strict and she wanted us to behave as adults and of course we didn't believe that. Teaching me those prayers brought out a softness in her that we never saw otherwise.

'At one level the clergy had very little contract with us apart from Mass on Sunday, and when they came to examine us in school on our religious doctrine. What we did have, though, was the stations. This meant having Mass in our home every so often. Everyone in the village took it in turns to have the stations and it was a great social and religious occasion. We all had a great sense of respect for it. I think it was very valuable and brought Mass into our homes, and that made it more relevant.

'I had pictures of St Teresa in my room. I always felt that St Teresa was a bit mine because of that. Maybe it's out of this mish-mash of things that we got our sense of God.'

The image of Jesus Alice acquired was of a loving and merciful man who showed the milk of human kindness, especially to those on the margins; a Saviour who came to call not the just but the sinners. Accusation and reprisal were the twin characteristics of the God of many of the preachers of her youth, not a compassionate healer but a grim reaper. Their God purified through terror. In spite of this, Alice retains a particular affection for the Redemptorists.

'My husband had an uncle who was in the Redemptorists and he was studying in Rome. When he was home on holidays he'd stay with us and he'd always bring us rosary beads. He was a very saintly and lovable man. When I was growing up the Redemptorists had a reputation for 'fire and brimstone', but we had a Redemptorist who used to visit our school and he was a very lovely man. I have two cousins, Denis and Pat O'Connor, who are Redemptorists. You judge an institution by the people you know. If you meet a German tourist you're inclined to judge all Germans by that one. I'm judging the Redemptorists on the basis of all those I know. I get on very well with my cousins, because of them I've a real soft spot for the Redemptorists.'

For all its problems, Alice is optimistic about the future of the Church in Ireland.

'In recent years the institution of the Church has changed a lot. When we were growing up in the country we found God in the fields, so we weren't dependent on the institution of the Church. Now that the institution of the Church has crumbled, the people are more aware that they are the Church and that God is within us all. I think we are going back now to a Church that is made up of a lot of small groups.

'Where I live now we have a prayer group every Monday night and there could be from ten to thirty people there. It is led by one of ourselves and it involves prayer and a reading from the Bible. The direction of the meeting is led by the person in charge of the night. We share our thoughts and our problems. We also have praise. At first it takes a bit of a time to get into praise but when you think about it, it's not God who needs our praise, it's we who need to praise God, because it liberates us. On some level, when we praise God or somebody else, it liberates something precious inside of us. We also have a little meditation group and we meet on a Friday morning. I think that is the path the Church is going to walk in the future. I think the journey we are going to walk is more of a private journey and less of an institutional journey.'

What does she think Jesus would say if he saw the state of Irish Christianity today?

'I think if Jesus was to come back today he'd say to us, "What have ye done to me?" Then I think he'd say, "Come back to me." Finally I think he'd say – which is very comforting – "Ye have begun the journey back to me".'

SINGING A NEW SONG

Eileen Reid

The anthem for the sixties generation was 'Hope I d-die before I get old'. Theirs was the generation that saw an unprecedented departure from previous generations. It was in the sixties that modern life as we know it today was shaped and moulded. It was the decade of the Beatles, pirate radio, monster peace-concerts, flower power and Mary Quant. Hope and idealism were the common currency. Nostalgically, everything about the time seems good, the concern for peace, the socially concerned songs of Bob Dylan and Joan Baez and the sense of freedom and optimism.

Higher educational standards, greater foreign travel and industrialisation opened the windows of change on Irish society. However, the greatest agent of social transformation was unquestionably the emergence of television; topics that had hitherto being shrouded in a veil of secrecy were openly discussed for the first time in pubs and parlours. New Year's Day 1962 was a watershed in Irish society when Ireland got its first television service. The first television sets began to trickle into homes a few months later. They were the latest of the never-ending miracles of science, those 'picture boxes' installed by the wealthier homeowners. They held children from their play and adults from their memories beside the fireside. The poorer families, who could not initially afford televisions, would almost beg to spend their evenings in those fortunate houses where the images flickered and came and went. The tenth commandment, 'Thou shalt not covet thy neighbours' goods', had never been broken so often before the televisions came to Ireland. Entertainment was never the same again. The little box in the corner made hostages of nearly all of us. People who we could never hope to meet became as real to us as family members because they were in our living rooms every evening.

While the Beatles were conquering the world, Ireland's equivalent was the showbands. The advent of the showband era brought great excitement to rural Ireland in particular. It also catapulted a new group of people, like Brendan Bowyer and Dickie Rock, to superstardom. Among the most distinctive of these new stars was Eileen Reid, who was lead singer with The Cadets from 1961-68. Her flamboyant hairstyle and her poignant tale of lost love 'I Gave My Wedding Dress Away' captivated music fans in halls throughout the country.

Eileen was reared in a religious family.

'I was brought up as a Catholic, but it was a real childlike approach. I always said prayers to my Guardian Angel. I left school when I was fourteen and I took the very basic teaching with me – like Jesus was born in a stable; the Virgin Mary; the Holy Spirit; and that Jesus died on the cross. In school, though, they never went into what the Bible says about particular issues. I grew up in a family that went to Mass every Sunday though we never said the rosary. That upbringing stayed with me and I went to Mass until I was twenty-five.'

Then, like many of her generation, she choose a different path. 'I got married in 1968 and I was in the band and all that and there was never once I stopped believing in God – never once. I knew he was in the tabernacle. End of story. But I didn't know him.

'I was an adulteress for fifteen years and I hadn't gone to Mass for fifteen years and I was inclined to row in with the way of the world. It's so easy to fall if you're not into Christ. He brought me back. God loves everyone and he will always bring them back. He hates the sin but he loves the sinner.'

It was her sister who was responsible for Eileen's spiritual rebirth.

'The Lord brought me back gently. I always knew that something was missing, but he rectified that. He just put a little noose around me and gradually dragged me back. A sister of mine used to go over to see Fr Aidan O'Carroll in the University Church on Wednesday nights and asked me one day, "Do you go to Mass?" I hadn't been to Mass for fifteen years, and there were even Christmasses when I missed Mass. I asked her what she did on Wednesday nights. She replied, "We're there for three hours." Of course I nearly fell through the floor. Then I asked her what they did for three hours in a chapel. She responded, "We say Mass and we say three rosaries." I told her, "I don't even say one rosary, how can you expect me to say three!" Now I love the rosary.

'I went over there one Wednesday and the place was packed and my sister, of course, horsed me over to the front seat and I sat there absolutely mortified for the night. My whole insides churned. It must have been because I was such a bad sinner. It was a torture for me. I wished a hole would open up and swallow me. I think I was the only one in the chapel who didn't receive communion.

'I went back four times in the month. I was very taken by Fr Aidan, who is a wonderful person and is especially fantastic when it comes to Bible readings. So I came home one night and I said to my husband, "Jimmy, I better get a Bible." I started on the New Testament and I began to read it in bed one night. It was like a loud bang went off in my head or that I had been struck by a bolt of lightning. All of a sudden I was confronted with the truth, truth, truth. I felt, "This is real." I was so enthralled that I was reading until five in the morning. I used to read the Bible at night time and I couldn't wait for the night to come so I could get stuck into it. Every single word in the Bible is true.

'We all need food to live, but in our busy lives and in our hectic world we also need spiritual food. I got great spiritual food from the Bible, but I also started to look for this spiritual food in other places. Mass once a week? To me, that's for the birds. I'll go once every day. In fact I'll go twice every day if I get the chance and if I had the time. The Mass is the greatest prayer.'

Eileen has the zeal of the convert when it comes to the Bible and attending Mass.

'God worked and turned my whole life around and it was through reading the Gospels. I feel that what God is saying is that there's an invite going out to everyone. No one is excluded. It doesn't matter how many terrible things you have done in the past. He's saying, "Come to me." Come into the chapel. He's in the Eucharist. The Eucharist is my life. The Mass is the big thing. The priest is blessed among men.'

Eileen's second time around love affair with God has turned her life on its head.

'The Lord said, "Only say the word and you shall be healed." Thanks be to God that's what he did for me. I've found peace in my heart and soul. I've no doubts whatsoever about my faith. I've been given the most wonderful blessing.

'I fell out of love with my husband but the Lord brought us back together in love again and now I love him deeply. How? It was through prayer. I let God run my life by taking him at his word. He said, "Put your life into my hands." I did and I fell madly in love with Jimmy again. Jesus came to fulfill the law of the prophets. I wanted the truth so I read the Gospels.'

Although her life is fulfilled and faith-filled, Eileen is worried about aspects of the Ireland of the third millennium.

'Sin has become that everything is all right and that something bad or wrong is not sin anymore. I especially worry about the young generation. I really pity kids today because they are not getting the example. We are all doing our own thing and we need somebody with a soft little rod to pull us back together. Where are the answers we need to live a good life? They are in the ten commandments.'

Eileen is like an old style missionary priest. Although her message is softer, she has that same passionate intensity about her religion.

'I'm still a sinner. Jesus came for sinners. You need Jesus Christ. He said, "Help me." He's so merciful and loving. He is love. He just said, "Ask me and you'll receive." All he is saying is, "Come to me." Try it. If you do you have everything to gain and if you don't you'll have everything to lose.'

SISTER OF MERCY

Sr Mary Killeen

Sr Mary Killeen has been described as Ireland's answer to Mother Teresa. It is not a comparison that sits comfortably with her. Yet it is an understandable analogy given the nature of her work. Her passion for the poor can be traced back to her childhood.

'I was born in Phibsboro and I was very much influenced by the Vincentians, who were a very vibrant force in the parish, and I was very impressed by their emphasis, which was like St Vincent de Paul, to help the poor.'

In her teenage years it was by no means inevitable that the woman destined to touch the lives of thousands of children would end up as a nun.

'When I was in primary school I was interested in becoming a nun, but when I went to secondary school that interest started to wane. I went to a school run by the Irish Sisters of Charity and they were very strict at the time. Although we were good students, at that age we weren't very impressed by their fondness for discipline.

'I went to Carysfort Training College, to train as a teacher after I left school, and during teacher training I was based in Cork Street, a very poor area. We saw the work the sisters were doing there with the children from broken homes or the children where the foster care system hadn't worked properly and were very impressed by their care. I felt kind of drawn to that sort of life, but at the same time I was half-thinking of marrying someone.

'During training college I got very sick. A girl came back to college with hepatitis and passed it on to me. I remember asking myself as I was sick: how would I like to die? So I promised myself that if I got better I was going to do something worthwhile with my life. That sickness had a huge effect on me, so I decided to become a sister. I didn't really want to be a nun but I felt it was something I should try and if it didn't work out then I would do something else.

'It was a big culture shock because the convent at the time had this grand Victorian lifestyle. There were aspects of it I liked, like the grand silence at nine o'clock at night so you had a time of contemplation.'

After eight or nine years teaching in Ireland, Sr Mary found that her superiors in the Sisters of Mercy had a surprise in store for her. 'I was asked to go to Kenya. I wasn't that keen. My father had just died and obviously it was not a time that I wanted to leave my mother to cope on her own, because it was a particularly tough time for her. I wasn't happy, but a sister in Kenya had become sick and she was the principal of a big Catholic school and they needed someone to replace her. I told them I wasn't thrilled at the prospect so they told me to think and pray about it. The next thing I knew they were presenting me with a ticket and visa!

'It was a big culture shock to be so far away and have no one you knew well to talk to. At the time it was very expensive to phone home. There was also the problem of living in a very different culture. The first few months I was numb from it all. I arrived on a Thursday and on the Monday morning I was head teacher of a primary school of over a thousand children. I was just barely thirty years old. The people were very nice and after a few months I began to really like the place.'

Surprisingly, the changes in religious practices that Sr Mary was initially exposed to were not as pronounced as might have been expected.

'When I went to Kenya first, I was dealing with the same sort of belief system that we have in Ireland, because the middle-class Churches in Nairobi were all run by Irish missionaries. But later on I moved to the slums.'

Sr Mary found herself in a tale of two cities.

'The city was divided by a river. On one side were the comfortable homes of the middle class and on the other were the slums. The poor started to cross the river and look for education. Our school was already crowded, but I got places for a hundred of them. They didn't mix in well with the existing students. They had no money for lunches. They were very hungry. They had no books and couldn't afford fees. I decided that if I was to really respond to their needs I would have to move to the slums. I was really, really shocked by what I saw and it affected me greatly. I saw that these people were living in the most horrific conditions. It beggared belief really.

'They also had no churches. We talk about the Church being the Church of the poor and that would make you laugh really. Here was a city with a million people living in houses and all the churches were there for them. Yet a million people were also living in the shanty towns where there wasn't a single church to be found. When I went to start an informal school in 1985 I built a hall where they could go to Mass on Sundays. When they went to Mass in the middle-class churches they were very poorly dressed and dusty, so they felt there was no welcome for them there. I felt it was no longer something I could do to go the slums, but something I should do.'

In Kenya, rural to urban migration is responsible for the high unemployment and the increased development of slums on the outskirts of the city of Nairobi. The cost of education, housing and healthcare is rising. Many children have no alternative but to roam the streets, exposed to crime, violence, drugs and prostitution. Some sixty thousand children (one in six being HIV positive) roam the streets of Kenya's capital city.

The Mukuru Centre, which Sr Mary founded, provides primary education for over four thousand street children, daily food of maize and beans for each child in the five schools, rehabilitation of new street children, a residential home for over one hundred orphans, a community development programme, social work and outreach to the slums, health education, post-primary skills training, and also sets up small businesses.

Under the leadership of Sr Mary, the project takes care of approximately six thousand street children, providing them with food, clothes, education and basic healthcare. It is an example of people living up to Jesus' challenge to his disciples in Matthew's Gospel: 'I was hungry and you fed me. I was thirsty and you gave me to drink. I was naked and you clothed me. I was a stranger and you welcomed me.'

It is shocking and horrifying that in this modern day children live in such terrible and unacceptable circumstances. Sr Mary has made it her life's mission to care for Kenya's forgotten children and to provide them with all the basic needs in life that we all take for granted; food and water, clothing, shelter, healthcare and education. A particular area of concern is to respond to the great need to build a skills centre for girls. Many African girls are neglected, with no hope of ever gaining a proper job. Sr Mary desperately wants to build a centre that will teach them the skills that will increase their chances of securing employment and give them the opportunity to become self-reliant.

'Theirs is a lost childhood and their only hope is the opportunity to go to school. The Mukuru Promotion Centre, under our stewardship, endeavours to help people to grow and to recognise their potential, and to offer the children in our care the opportunity to become self-respecting, self-reliant adults, capable of effecting positive change in society.

'As Sisters of Mercy we are challenged by our foundress, Catherine MacAuley, to work alongside the poor and to empower them to live with dignity, satisfying their need for food, healthcare, clothing, housing and education. As Catherine MacAuley always said, the poor need help today, not next week.

'We are all children of God. Some churches are very middle class and they expel those who are ragged. We try to make sure that those with nothing get something. I see God as the father or mother of us all – a loving, compassionate God. This is a God who challenges the comfortable. It is a God who challenges each one of us to reach out to people in need and those on the margins as Jesus himself did.'

If you would like to help Sr Mary in her work, her address is: Sister of Mercy DKA Office, PO Box 17699, Nairobi, Kenya.

TRUE BELIEVER?

Joseph O'Connor

As a teenager, Joe O'Connor first emerged on the national stage when he began writing for newspapers and *Magill*. He then went on to scale the heights of the literary world with a series of best-selling books. His most recent novel *Inishowen* rocketed to the top of the best-seller list in its first week of publication. As a child and young teenager he was very interested in religion and seriously contemplated joining the priesthood.

'No one in my family became a priest or a nun and, possibly for that reason, I am always very impressed by priests and nuns. I was a very religious child and young teenager. I was educated by the Holy Ghost Fathers in Blackrock, many of whom were wonderful men. I was particularly interested in the idea of the missionary orders and I was very serious about it, but then I changed my mind.'

While Joe was lost to the priesthood, he feels that there are many parallels with the priest and the writer.

'I think so much of religion is to do with the "word". If you read the Scriptures the imagery of words and language reoccurs very frequently in the Gospels, "I am the Word" and "in the beginning was the Word". The people who wrote the Gospels were very conscious of the iconography of language. I think it is a very good skill for a preacher or a minister of any kind to have. We share with priests the fact that we live or die by our ability to use the language.'

Joe's family background has been the subject of much comment, largely because of the comments of his outspoken and often controversial sister, Sinead. How much truth is in the public image of his childhood?

'I am always very careful, when I talk of this, to specify that it is amazing how people who go through exactly the same set of experiences perceive them to be different and it is very important that their perception be respected. I wouldn't deny many of the things my sister said in public. It was certainly a very painful and difficult upbringing. Where I feel enough credit isn't always given is to my father, who was really a very wonderful parent and a very loving man, ahead of his time in some ways in that he didn't suffer from the Irish male thing of not being able to express love. We were always told we were loved from when we were very young. I feel that sometimes not enough credit is given to people who did do their best and who really were very unusual in some ways.'

Joe himself has embraced marriage.

'I was thirty-five and I didn't just jump in. It was a carefully thought out decision. My own parents' marriage wasn't very happy. I remember very clearly, at the age of eight or nine, deciding that I wouldn't get married until the age of forty, but anyway, the wonderful wife I have persuaded me to do it five years earlier. My wife is a practising Catholic and I am not, so you will appreciate that the whole business of how we would get married was very difficult, but we eventually got married twice, once in the registry office and then in the church, so you could say I am the most married person! It was a strange experience. We were both very conscious of what words would be used and very conscious of the finality. I am always amazed when people say that being married doesn't make any difference, it's just a piece of paper. I found the day both emotional and spiritually enriching.

'I don't think you could even call the service in the registry office a ceremony, although to me it was very important and meaningful, as it only takes ten minutes. It's kind of brief and to the point, but I suppose it's the only kind of legal wording that includes the word "love". That was impressive.

'I was very glad, though, that we also did the religious ceremony, because I believe that the future in this country lies in the bringing of people together. I don't think the notion that Ireland should be divided between believers and non-believers is a particularly useful distinction. For someone like me who would come from the perspective of agnosticism, on a good day, these things derive a sacredness from the fact that other people find them sacred. I think it's very important to remember that. You can have a humanist position that absolutely respects the fact that the miraculous is often embodied in the day to day lives of other people and the fact that you don't perceive God in the same way, if at all, shouldn't be as important as the fact that they do. I was very glad that we did it for that reason.'

The twinkle in Joe's eyes reveals that he is not really serious when he claims that his difficulties with the Church began at an early age.

'My sister, Sinead, was born on 8th December, the feast of the Immaculate Conception. Because it was a feast day, and my mother was in hospital, my granny took me to Mass in Glasthule Church. I would have been about four or five then. We arrived late for Mass and the church was absolutely packed. We were standing at the back. We came to communion time. My father had been holding me in his arms and he gave me to my granny and went up, got communion and came back down. My granny gave me to my father, went up, got Communion and came back down. The priest started to put the chalice and the rest away. I suddenly became incensed and started bawling at the top of my five-year-old lungs as loud as I possibly could, "He's putting it all away and I didn't get any." My grandmother was a daily communicant and was extremely embarrassed by this. I feel that's the beginning of my difficult relationship with the Church. If only I'd got communion on that day!'

Joe O'Connor is a fascinating mixture of the humorous and the serious. He wanders back and forth between these two worlds with ease. He has a keen interest in social issues, national and international, and is disturbed by some aspects of the 'Celtic Tiger'.

'There are enormous inequalities in Irish society generally. That the numbers living in poverty are far too high in a society that is achieving so much economically is one thing that bothers me.'

Although Joe professes to be an agnostic, religion is a recurring theme in his writing. One of his collection of short stories was called *True Believers*.

'Depending on how you define the word, I would consider myself a very religious writer. One of my novels, *Desperadoes*, is set in Nicaragua and is about a middle-aged Irish couple who are separated. Their son, in his twenties, has gone to Nicaragua and has been reported dead. They have to go there to find him. The entire novel was really inspired by a reading of the various versions of the Magi story. I am very interested in the Magi story as the ultimate metaphor for faith.

'My second last novel, *The Salesman*, was about a very religious idea. It's about the idea of forgiving your enemy, is that possible? Is Christ's injunction to "turn the other cheek" a good idea? Is it psychologically possible, and if so, how would you do it? What implications would it have? We take these truths simply because the Judaeo-Christian culture is so pervasive. We can all spout that stuff, we can all say if you have two coats you should give one to your brother. We all know these things, but we never think about them. I think that often people with an atheistic or agnostic point of view think about religious ideas far more deeply than people who are religious do.

'I think Oscar Wilde is probably a good person to invoke, as he experienced a very fervent death-bed conversion to Catholicism, which, if I am in any fit state to do, I will be doing myself. If there is any free insurance going I will be having it! I have always been very interested in the characterisations, from a literary point of view almost, of the disciples. I find them very fascinating people, and of course the most fascinating person to me is the patron saint of the agnostic, St Thomas. You can conceive of the twelve personalities, from the tiny fragments we have of them, almost as a whole human personality; various facets of one person, one holistic being, and St Thomas is there for a very good reason, God is saying it's okay to doubt, we cannot all be believers. And I think the reason he is there is to say, "Even you won't be excluded". Just as the believer has moments of doubt, the agnostic has moments of belief.'

IT COULD HAPPEN TO A BISHOP

Christopher Jones

'Are you really a bishop?' A young boy with special needs is sceptically checking out the credentials of the Bishop of Elphin, Christopher Jones. The boy is bemused and disarmed by his informality and lack of airs and graces before a children's liturgy.

Born in Rathcroghan in Tulsk, County Roscommon, the youngest of a family of eleven, Bishop Jones sums up his childhood as 'healthy, happy and wholesome'. His early life was dominated by farming and football, punctuated by trips to the cinema in Roscommon on Friday nights.

He entered Maynooth as a seminarian in 1955, following his brother into the priesthood. Three of his sisters also entered religious life.

'I was aware of being very fortunate to come from a happy home. I wanted to respond to that by giving my life to God in the priesthood. After I was ordained in 1962 I wrote to my bishop asking for permission to go to South America, only to receive a reply, which did not mention my request, informing me that the Bishop of Kilalla had a vacancy for a priest and that I was to write to him to offer my services.'

He promptly took up a teaching position in St Muirdeach's in Ballina before returning to his alma mater in Summerhill where he taught for six years. After a short time as archivist in St Mary's in

37

Sligo, he was sent back to university to study social science with a view to upgrading the social services in Sligo.

'We started in 1973, providing a vast range of services such as meals on wheels, marriage counselling and special services for alcoholics and the homeless and all the kind of services that were needed.'

In 1979 he took on an additional responsibility by becoming a curate in Rosses Point.

'Initially I thought I wouldn't be able to double up with the two jobs, but a few of my friends suggested that I should take the post because I was seeing all the problems of life and that I needed to balance that by seeing some of the more positive side of life like happy marriages. They were right.'

In 1987 he was appointed as administrator to the cathedral in Sligo and seven years later it was announced that he was to become Bishop of Elphin. How did he react to the news?

'I didn't expect that I would be asked. When I did get the phone call from the Papal Nuncio I was very surprised. It was, in many ways, a very frightening call to have to take on such responsibility. It makes you look very carefully at your own life and your own unworthiness for such a place in the Church.'

It was a big adjustment for him to make, especially because some people put him up on a pedestal.

'One of the great supports in my life as priest was the love of the people I served. Irish people know their priest very well and if you're decent with them they'll treat you well. Being a bishop you find yourself a bit isolated. You're meeting people on a more superficial level. What I miss most is that tangible sense of the people's support that you get in a parish. When you are a bishop, people and priests, unless they are close friends, do not get as close to you and don't feel as free in what they can say when you're around. I miss the closeness that I would have experienced with people in the community.'

Having been appointed bishop in 1994, he was immediately confronted by the scandals that swept the Church.

'At the time I became a bishop, the Church was rocked by the news that priests had been responsible for the sexual abuse of children. I often think that if the Church had asked a committee to design a programme that would do it the maximum damage it couldn't have come up with anything more damaging. The scandals were highlighted by the media. I believe that if somebody commits a crime they should be punished fully, but I have this tremendous horror of that story being told and retold and of the damage that does to their victims. I would question why these criminals' stories have to be told and told again.'

Given his work in social services, Bishop Jones has a particular interest in justice issues. Like his colleague Willie Walsh, he has strong views on the treatment of Travellers.

'I did work with Travellers. I was secretary of the National Council for ten years and I was chairman until 1991. There's a thousand Traveller families on the side of the road and they are there simply because so many people are opposed to having Travellers live near them. Through my work I got to know Travellers and visit them on their campsites and camps and I discovered that they are a beautiful people with a beautiful culture of their own and, generally speaking, have great fidelity in their married lives.

'I feel we have marginalised them. We hear so much about the third world and it's on our own doorstep. I know that people get upset because they see dirty sites, but the only reason there are dirty sites is that the County Council or people like that don't collect litter. They're not recognising that legal right. Such Travellers have no running water, litter collection or electricity. They are dirty because of our neglect and our refusal to provide them with conditions which give them proper human dignity.'

Another concern is the way the socio-economic system unintentionally undermines family life.

'The whole concept of marriage is being corroded by a social policy that makes it more economically attractive for a woman to have children outside marriage.'

Bishop Jones feels passionately that the Church must be actively involved in working for a just society.

'The first right is the right to life. Once you accept that, you accept a lot of other rights: education, accommodation, health, etc. When you look around, you see that in our society many people are being denied these rights. I really believe that we have failed our poor in Ireland by not providing them with education. Somebody said once that socialism provided an equal opportunity for people to be unequal. We don't even have that, an equal opportunity for all to have a proper education, that to me is the one key to open the prison of poverty.

'The other big area of inequality is health. I'm a member of the VHI, so that if I need an operation for a hip or something I can go straight into hospital and have one, but there are other people in the town I live in who don't have VHI, who have to wait for a year or more for even a minor operation.'

Given this preoccupation with justice, it is hardly surprising that his heroes and heroines share that conviction.

'Mother Teresa was a great inspiration to me. She came to visit Sligo a few years ago. I know it was one of the great moments of my life to meet her. She had such energy and yet was so frail.

'I also greatly admire Jean Kennedy-Smith, who I think is very under-rated for what she has done in the peace process in terms of involving the American administration. Tony Blair is another person I greatly appreciate. He has shown great integrity in his dealings in Northern Ireland and is a man of deep spirituality. John Hume was a class ahead of me in Maynooth. His whole life has been spent in the community and in the service of peace. I think we should celebrate men like that.

'I have tremendous admiration for the example of Archbishop Helder Camara. He actually lived in a little sacristy of his cathedral in Brazil. When I visited the country, any time I mentioned his name I was greeted by a smile. He took very unpopular stands. One of the things he said to me was: "When I gave food to the poor everybody called me a saint. When I asked why were people poor everybody called me a communist." They punished him severely for that, but he showed tremendous courage.'

Is there a lesson for the Church in Ireland in that?
'The more the Church is involved in the search for justice the more respect we will have. We must stand with the poor.'

How does Bishop Jones evaluate the state of the Church in the early years of the new millenium?

'The Church has suffered a lot because of recent scandals, but I think we have been purified by our suffering. On a national level, there is a lot of cynicism about the Church, fuelled by many in the media. My experience, though, is that people at local level who have enjoyed the service of their priest are still very loyal to the Church.

'I think in the future we will see a Church that is humbler, more tolerant, more forgiving and more transparent. I'm very confident about the future. Our numbers may not be as big, but I think it will be a healthier and more vibrant Church.'

FOR GOD'S SAKE

Walton Empey

Dramatic chance encounters are normally the stuff of Hollywood, but not so for the Church of Ireland Archbishop of Dublin, Bishop of Glendalough and Primate of Ireland. The course of Walton Empey's life was transformed by a chance meeting with a sailor. Up to that meeting he was adamant he would never become a clergyman. The change of heart came about one Christmas Day when he was a student at Trinity College:

'My father was a Church of Ireland priest before me, I loved him dearly and he was marvellous, but everyone used to say to you as a young fellow, "No doubt you will be a clergyman like your father". Many children in this position find it extremely irritating. I found it very annoying and therefore didn't really consider it very seriously.

'I was acting as a voluntary worker with the Mission for Seamen and was called for duty at Christmas because a number of staff were sick. I had arrived with less than good grace as I was due to play an important rugby match two days later and I was going to miss that. I was working around the port and was walking the SouthWall in the evening. I noticed a ship with no watchman. I knew there ought to be one somewhere. I went down and I saw a faint light under the mess door. I can still picture him so vividly – a black sailor with white, white hair, startlingly white, and he was sitting down to his

Christmas meal of a boiled egg and a cup of tea. He was all on his own and the loneliness in that dirty little steamer was pretty awful.

'Through the good offices of the Mission, not through me, we managed to get him down for his Christmas dinner and provision was made for a watchman. I will never forget the joy on his face. He never had a Christmas like it. Those things made me think a little bit more, in fact an awful lot more, about what I ought to be doing.'

The future Archbishop of Dublin would have a further reason to recall his days in the mission. He married a woman who was a volunteer there! After his ordination he spent two years as a curate of St Paul's Glenageary before he and Louisa got married. On the day after their wedding they sailed for a six-year posting in Canada. They returned to Ireland in 1966 and five years later Dr Empey became Dean of Limerick. While he enjoyed the new position immensely, there was a personal cost to be paid. Like many people before and since he found that a particularly busy time in his career coincided with the formative years of his children.

'I was made Dean of Limerick and Rector of Limerick city parish, which is a sprawled-out parish with an enormous number of chaplaincies, schools, hospitals, a prison, and so on. The day was extremely full and often I would be gone in the morning before the kids went to school, and then maybe back in the evening after they had gone to bed. It was my wife who bore the burden.'

In Limerick he established a reputation as an enthusiastic ecumenist. The passage of time has in no way diminished his passion for this subject.

'It's extremely important to me. All the Churches in Ireland are facing difficulties and undergoing hard times, and the more we can do together, the better it is for everyone. We are all called to be one. Let's not forget that this was part of Our Lord's prayer the night before he died, that we should be all one.

'It doesn't mean uniformly one, boringly one, but it does mean that to be fighting with one another is totally contrary to the will of

Christ for his Church. The more we can do together, the better it is. I think many young people are rightly turned off when they see the Churches squabbling from time to time and then they just get completely turned off and say a plague on all of your houses. There are difficulties, but they are not as important as the things we agree about.

'In ecumenical matters, particularly at local level, there has been a vast change throughout the years. From being considered as nothing other than heretics by the Roman Catholic Church in earlier days, we are now in a much happier situation. Although we still have considerable difficulties in such areas as interchurch marriage and intercommunion to name but two, relationships have vastly improved. Many of our churches in sparsely populated areas simply would not be able to exist without the financial aid and encouragement given by Roman Catholic neighbours.'

Archbishop Empey is particularly happy that ecumenism has at last spread its tentacles into Irish sporting matters.

'I grew up in Wexford in the 1950s and my passion was rugby. It was during the era of the great Wexford hurling team of Nicky Rackard, Paudge Kehoe, etc, and I used to go to watch them train. There was a ban on then, you couldn't play rugby and GAA, so I couldn't play hurling. But I used to look at it and marvel at the beauty and skill of it, my mouth watered. Sadly by the time the ban was lifted I was too old to do anything about it.'

Despite his warm, genial personality, Walton Empey is not afraid to take a stand on controversial issues, from Orange marchers to divorce and women priests. He has not been afraid to publicly change his position. In 1978 he resigned from a select committee on the ordination of women to the priesthood. Later, though, he had a change of heart.

'I had to come a long way on that one but I'm extremely pleased about it. We can't afford to sit back on our laurels there and say, we've done our bit. At our general synod I had to sit on a chair way up there and look down at the elected people from every diocese in Ireland and the sprinkling of women was very small indeed. We've got a long way to go yet.'

Archbishop Empey has the unique distinction of being the only Church of Ireland bishop to have served in the Defence Forces. As a young man he served in the FCA in Enniscorthy for four years, leaving as a three-star Private in 1957. He has made several visits to the Lebanon to see Irish peace-keeping troops.

'As we speak, Irish soldiers are serving in a dangerous and sensitive role of peace-keeping in Southern Lebanon, trying, with other nations, to preserve a thin blue line between two violent antagonists. When they went there in 1979 they were the second battalion to arrive and they have been there ever since. Over thirty soldiers have died there on peace-keeping missions. If they were involved in a war of aggression this would be a small number, but it's very significant in terms of peace-keeping.'

Archbishop Empey has been very troubled by the misconceptions some people have about the Church of Ireland.

'Since my election as Archbishop of Dublin I have been asked many times about the Church of Ireland and politics. Within ten minutes of confirmation of my election I was asked a question on the lines of: "Could you comment on the increasing perception that the Church of Ireland is the Unionist party at prayer?" To say that I was taken aback would be the understatement of the week. We belong to a Church without a border; we reflect in our membership many different strands of Church life – Evangelical, High Church and liberal; we reflect a wide variety of political opinion from Nationalist to Unionist and a variety of shades in between; we reflect every class in society and a wide variety of cultural backgrounds. But we are one Church – we are one Church and we try to be faithful to the Christian Gospel as "this Church has received it" despite all our diversity.

'The Church of Ireland of my youth was still a Church that

largely kept its head behind parapets. However, thankfully this is no longer the case. Those of us who live in the State love our country, warts and all, and that point needs stressing again and again. For the most part, our criticisms of government would be the same as our fellow Roman Catholic citizens rather than as simply members of the Church of Ireland. We have found a renewed confidence in the past twenty-five years or so. We speak out when necessary on issues of the day and, what is more, we are listened to. Apart from some extremists who are always with us, we are accepted as loyal citizens of this State who are not looking backwards wistfully to a time that was. At every level of Irish social life members of the Church are playing their part right up to Dáil representation.'

Although the challenge facing him is formidable, he has no doubt what is required of him.

'I was ordained to be a pastor, to be a priest. That was my first love. That's why I came into the ministry. And I never ceased being a priest just because I'm an archbishop. The clergy are forever pastoring other people and it is a difficult time in which to be a priest. Things are changing very quickly and great demands are made upon them, and it is essential that they too have a pastor, someone they can go to, someone they can talk to about their difficulties. I feel this is vital.'

THE MEMORY MAN

Jimmy Magee

The great sports commentators share a magical capacity to raise and refresh the spirit and to heighten the quality of human perception. Jimmy Magee is one of them. His is a world of wonder, admiration and enchantment. The bond he forged with the radio and television audience may be ephemeral but is nonetheless real for that.

The credibility he enjoys with all Irish sports fans, including the many whose only experience of big games is via television, is reward for the width and depth of his involvement in sport. He is as much part of the furniture of our lives as Riverdance and political scandals. His feel for the heartbeat of sport – the ripple of excitement that does not communicate itself to everybody, but puts those it reaches permanently in thrall – permeates every word he utters.

Sport's hold on him has obviously been strengthened over the years by the extraordinary access his job has given him to its most compelling performers, and by the licence it has given him to enjoy thousands of adventure playgrounds all over the globe. Many of them have been dazzling. If he tried to compile a list of those that thrilled him to the core, the names would spill over many a page. Alongside Christy Ring, Mick O'Connell, Pele and all the other greats, there would be a number of much more obscure names whose lack of celebrity did not prevent them from brightening at least one day of his life. He cites seeing Barry McGuigan becoming world champion in 1985 as the highlight of his career as a commentator, with American super-athlete Carl Lewis' extraordinary performance, winning four Olympic Gold medals at the one games, as a close second.

He lists a litany of famous names that he has interviewed – a virtual who's who of world sport. Each of them had a story to tell. To take one example, Arthur Ashe who in 1975 defeated reigning champion Jimmy Connors to claim the Wimbledon title. He had his first heart attack at the age of thirty-six. He underwent bypass surgery then, and again four years later. As recovery from his second operation was particularly slow, he agreed to receive a few extra units of blood as a boost. Five years later, his right hand went limp. Emergency surgery revealed the cause: AIDS.

Resilience and strong principles were Ashe's trademarks, as was evident in his childhood when his mother died. His father sat on his son's bed, weeping as he told him the news. The boy answered: 'Don't cry, Daddy. As long as we have each other we'll be all right.' They were also to the forefront in his final days.

After keeping his illness a secret, he went public about it in April 1992 when he learned that a newspaper intended to print a story about his condition. Despite being weak from the illness, he continued his lifelong work helping children, working to give a haven to Haitian refugees, fighting racial injustice and battling AIDS. Right up to the very end he maintained that the biggest problem he had to endure in life was not AIDS but racial prejudice. Throughout his adult life he sought to bring blacks and whites together.

Asked before he died if he felt cheated, Ashe answered: 'Death doesn't frighten me. If I asked "Why me?" about my troubles, I would have to ask "Why me?" about my blessings. "Why my winning Wimbledon? Why my marrying a beautiful, gifted woman and having a wonderful child?"'

Almost before he has time to catch his breath, Jimmy has moved on to talking about a more local hero.

'One of my favourite characters in sport is Clare's Ger Loughnane. There've been so many stories told about him and the lengths he has gone to to win matches in recent years. I'm sure that he smiles to himself when he hears them. In 1995 I had all my childhood dreams come true when I commentated, live on UTV, on my first All-Ireland final. I was in absolute heaven. Clare won the match and over the next few years I had a lot of contact with Ger in a professional capacity. I always found him incredibly helpful and co-operative and never demanding in any way.'

Despite his long involvement in print journalism, Jimmy's fame rests mainly on the spoken word. His voice can stay calm and mellifluous, and deliver the relevant information in the most thrilling contest – the perfect instrument for putting names and personalities to the blurred rainbow of a heart-stopping match. Such is his mastery of facts and figures that one fan was prompted to say, 'the bugger is never wrong.'

Although his career as a commentator has brought him many highs, Jimmy Magee has also plunged into deep tunnels and dark places.

'I don't want to sound like I'm doing the poor mouth and I'm not looking for sympathy, but I've had a rough dozen years or so. It all began when my wife died. That was a shattering blow to me. My mother died as well.

'Then I had one of the darkest and most difficult periods in my life. There's a story going around that I collapsed in an airport and was rushed to hospital. That's total nonsense. It was nothing as dramatic as that. What had been happening was that I was going over to England every weekend, for RTÉ's coverage of the Premiership on Saturday nights, to commentate on a soccer match. Inevitably, to get up to the commentary position you have to make a climb up a ladder. I found that this was taking more and more out of me and I had to leave half an hour earlier than I used to – to negotiate some of these climbs, like the one at Aston Villa, so that I wouldn't be completely out of breath when the match started. It was something I tried to ignore for as long as I could.

'Then, after chatting to my doctor one day, I found myself having a consultation with Maurice Nelligan, whose name will be familiar to most Irish people because of his prominence in the field. I was supposed to be going to Nottingham that Saturday to commentate on Notts Forest's match with Manchester United. Maurice said to me, "I can't make you do what you don't want to, but you're a great man for statistics and the statistics suggest that if you don't have surgery you're going to die." That's not really the kind of thing you want to be told.

'Instead of seeing Manchester United, I agreed to open-heart surgery and it seems to have worked out okay in the end, though there were a lot of complications because of problems with some of my other organs. The fact of the matter was that before I had surgery I had to face up to the realities of the situation and be ready to die – and I was.'

How did he go about it?

'I had to make my peace with God. I was brought up as a Catholic like most Irish people of my generation. I'm not exceptionally religious. I'm not one for Lough Derg nor Lourdes nor anything like that, but God was always there, somewhere or other in my life. I didn't have a death-bed conversion or any visions. I was able, though, to talk with God myself and be prepared if he was going to take me with him.'

The post-operation Jimmy is a much slimmed down model.

'I lost twenty-five pounds in two weeks. I have found the secret of diet, although at the time I was too sick to worry about my figure I can assure you, and it all happened by accident. For two weeks in hospital I lived on nothing only jelly and Seven-Up and that's what lost the weight for me.'

Was his brush with mortality a watershed in his life?

'The one thing an experience like that does is to put things in perspective. When your life is nearly snatched away from you, you start to realise what really matters and to be grateful for what you have rather than complaining about what you're missing out on.

'Some time after my surgery I was talking to Kevin O'Brien, the great Wicklow player. He is one of the best players in the modern game but — because he is with a weaker county in football terms — he has not had the success he deserves. I asked him how he coped with the disappointment and he told me that he was involved with some of the Kosovo refugees and compared to what they went through his disappointments in football are inconsequential.

'The one thing I will say is that once you are alive and you have half-decent health there's always, always someone worse off than you.'

THROUGH THE BARRICADES

Richard Moore

On 30th January 1972, British paratroopers shot twenty-six anti-internment marchers on the streets of Derry, killing fourteen and wounding many. The day became known as Bloody Sunday. It marked a watershed in the unfolding history of the province. Internment had been introduced the previous August by the increasingly desperate Unionist regime at Stormont. It was a blunt instrument and doomed to failure. The operation was bungled, with many cases of mistaken identity among those arrested. It was a straightforwardly sectarian and one-sided act, a political ploy to appease the Unionist politicians. It was complemented by sophisticated interrogation techniques by the army – notably sensory deprivation – and allegedly a good deal of unsophisticated brutality. The anti-internment marches were a gesture of protest against a failed system and against the increasingly brutal minds that accompanied its policies. Such was the reaction to Bloody Sunday that within two months the Stormont parliament was dissolved and direct rule instituted. Westminster assumed full responsibility for all other functions of government in the six counties.

When the troubles started in 1969, they had come second only to the weather as the main topic of conversation. But gradually the public had become anaesthetised to the slaughter. Reports of the casualties became a notorious turn-off, causing a glazing of the eyes and a furrowing of brows. Bloody Sunday was different. It seemed to touch a deep nerve with everybody.

As a ten-year-old in Derry, Richard Moore's family were directly affected by this atrocity. His uncle, Gerard McKinney, aged thirty-five, was going to the assistance of a wounded man when he saw a British soldier in the alleyway. He raised his arms and shouted, 'Don't shoot! Don't shoot!' The autopsy report on McKinney supported the eye-witness claims that he had his hands in the air when shot. He left behind seven young children. A week after he was buried, his wife, Ita, gave birth to their eighth child, a baby boy whom she named Gerard.

Quite unbelievably, William McKinney (no relation), aged twenty-six, ran to the aid of Gerard. As he bent over his namesake, he was shot in the back and killed. Richard has very vivid memories of that day.

'I remember the silence that fell on Derry then. It was something out of the ordinary. I was out playing with my friends and suddenly I noticed my uncle calling to the house and later more relatives. Then I saw my mother was crying and she told me that her brother, Gerard, had been shot. It was very hard on her, but I don't think any of us will ever appreciate exactly how tough the whole thing was for his wife Ita.

'The other thing I remember most about Bloody Sunday was the funerals. I don't think I'll ever forget coming into the church and looking up to see the thirteen coffins laid out side by side. That is a sight I will take with me to my grave.'

Four months later, on 4th May, the troubles cast an even deeper shadow on Richard's young life.

'I was walking home from school one day at twenty past three in the afternoon, I walked past a British Army look-out post, I remember passing it and that's all I remember. I found out later that a soldier let off his gun and I was struck by a rubber bullet in the head from about ten feet. I got hit in the bridge of my nose. I lost one eye and the other was rendered useless. I was taken away and laid out on a table in the school and a teacher who knew me very well saw me and didn't recognise me because my face was so badly damaged. I remember being taken away, and the siren of the ambulance. My father was with me in the ambulance. He wouldn't let my mother see me because he didn't want her to see me in that condition.

'I'm sure when my mother heard about Bloody Sunday and Gerard she thought that was probably the end of it for her family. But four months later the Troubles landed right smack back in the middle of their living room again, and I was blinded for life because of that bullet. My mother and father were good, God-fearing people. They went to Mass every day. They never talked about politics and all of a sudden they had to face this double tragedy. My parents prayed a lot and it must have been prayer that got us through it. It could have been nothing else. When I learned that I would never see again I cried that I would never see my Mammy and Daddy again.'

Unlike many of his contemporaries he did not give in to bitterness.

'I'm not bitter. I bear no ill will towards the soldier who shot me and in fact I would like to meet him and tell him that. Bitterness is a destructive emotion and only hurts the person who is bitter.

'Make no mistake, I have paid a heavy price for what happened to me on that day in 1972. I am married now and I have two daughters. I was there for their births and I would have given anything to be able to see what they looked like. Likewise, one of them has made her first Holy Communion. I was there for it but I would've loved to have been able to see it. Christmas morning as they open their Christmas presents I would love to be able to see the smiles on their faces. So all those pleasures have been denied to me. I have lost a lot, but I can forgive that soldier.'

Sadly, Richard's forgiveness has been the rare exception in the history of the Northern conflict. A traumatic period of the type not seen since Bloody Sunday was triggered off with the beginning of the hunger strikes by the H-Block protesters. The name of Bobby Sands was on everyone's lips. The image of martyrdom, of a group of young men willing to sacrifice themselves for their cause even to the point of a painful death, touched a deep chord with all people, north and south, with the slightest nationalist sympathies.

There was a very definite religious flavour to these events. This was reflected in language like 'hungering and thirsting after justice' that brought into stark focus the twin notions of sacrificial suffering and the imperative of opposing and overcoming injustice in the community. It was the politics of the gut. Critical faculties, though not discarded, were often seriously neglected. The dark shadow of Irish history, north and south, had created too easy a toleration of political violence.

The hunger strikes unleashed, with great ferocity, the potent cocktail of politics and religion that has made Irish history such a complicated mess. In the south, the Catholic majority were unable to watch the situation from a detached position because of the latent religious – and specifically Catholic – motifs. Republican ideology frequently stressed the redemptive power of suffering. On the occasion of the death of an IRA activist, death notices often referred to the claim that: 'It is not those who inflict the most, but those who suffer the most, who will have the final victory.' Great play was made on the image of the individual and the whole Catholic community as victim, heroically enduring a sacrificial suffering. At one point in the late seventies the IRA sought to have an advertisement published in the *Irish News* that depicted a crucified and bleeding figure on a cross, wearing the distinctive black beret of the organisation. For their part, the Protestant community tended to compare themselves to the people of Israel in biblical times, beset on all sides by the enemy.

Richard's main flashpoint is not the number of problems, nor the scale of the problems, but our collective failure to do anything to solve them. When action is called for, too often we simply respond with platitudes. When confronted with problems we simply wash our hands like Pontius Pilate. His anger is not with our actions, but with our non-actions, by our collective sins of omission. He points out that if we are not part of the solution we are part of the problem.

In the Ireland of today there are three possible responses for us. We might be prophets announcing the better age to come. Alternatively we could be preservers making sure that in the flux of life the validity of past insights will not be lost. Richard embodies a third approach: to share the drama of the age and work for the advancement of society and of the common good.

In partnership with Concern International, Richard has established and directs the ecumenical 'Children in Crossfire', an organisation to build bridges between the two communities. Rather than remaining a prisoner of history, he is at the frontier of shaping a new future in Northern Ireland where the traditional enmities are redundant.

'No one knows better the damage the Troubles have caused than I do. I carry it with me every moment of my life in a very real way. If I can forgive, why can't others do the same?'

THE SLAUGHTER OF THE INNOCENTS

Peter Paul McGinley

There are no words to adequately describe the bloodbath that has taken place in former Yugoslavia, where society appears to have been drawn into a web of ever-increasing intolerance, bigotry and racial tension. The international community has largely responded by not responding.

It is often said that the first casualty of war is the truth, but whose truths? Such is the complexity of the conflict that it is difficult, if not impossible, to identify the 'good guys' and 'bad guys'. In the thousands of articles that have attempted to analyse the source of the conflict and the search for a political or military solution, the human cost of the war sometimes does not get the attention it deserves. Such is the enormity of the horror that it is virtually impossible for any eye-witness to speak dispassionately about the topic.

A recent visitor to Ireland to raise awareness of the ongoing problems in the area was Peter Paul McGinley, a Croatian of Scottish descent. I spoke to him about his experiences.

'The Serbian tanks first appeared on the streets in May 1991. At that stage we didn't know we were at war. It was only when the tanks surrounded our Croatian town, with a population of just forty-four thousand, that we knew we were in a war situation. We had no army and virtually no communication with the outside world. Within a few months we had run out of food. We had only grass to eat. If you were lucky you had fried dog food and grass. If you are starving to death it tastes very good. On 15th November of that year we surrendered. We were starved. We were marched out at gunpoint and then the slaughter began. The Jewish population no longer exists there. It was total extermination.

'After we surrendered, the torture began immediately. There was a massacre all the way as the troops advanced. The people were separated into three groups: men, women and children. The men were all killed. The women were raped. It was impossible to keep up with all the killing. I've heard people since talking about ethnic cleansing. This is not a Serb term but a media phrase. It is a nice way of saying extermination.

'We were put in what were called internment camps. In reality, they were concentration and slave labour camps. In my case they took my fingernails out and burned me with cigarettes. Their tactic was to kill people in the cruellest way possible – piece by piece. They sliced people up, cut off their noses, then stopped, cut off the lips, then stopped, cut off the fingers, stopped again, then the eyes were cut out and they stopped again. They used stop-start tactics in their torture because there was more pain that way. When they got tired they killed people.

'The television cameras showed a mass grave of five thousand people. That's extermination. In one building they put nine hundred people and took their knives into it and did their business. Another time, they put three hundred people in a field and did the same. I saw two ten-year-old girls running into a building in search of safety. The soldiers hurled a flame-thrower into the building and burned them alive. I saw one little boy being raped and they put bayonets through his eyes.

'They forced us to dig our own graves and while we were digging they continued to torture people just for the fun of it, but by the end they were very drunk. When we were put into the graves they started shooting, but sometimes the bullets went over the intended victims' heads. I was one of the few lucky ones who fell into that category and when darkness fell I was able to crawl out and make my escape. It's a blur now.'

He had to become accustomed to the sight of old men, thin as broomsticks, nothing more than skin and bones, crawling on all fours; children with bellies as large as pregnant women's, their limbs like matchsticks. Mothers, going without food themselves, had to watch their children starving to death in the most hideous way imaginable. The scale of the suffering and sorrow left the people trembling and sick. The immediate impact was awful. People lay in agony, uncontrollable bodies shook and shuddered, and the stench of human excrement and vomit stunned the senses. The helpless masses, herded into sheds, could but sit and wait. For many, death was a release. The people were normally woken to the agony of another day, as dawn struggled to extract the first rays of heat, by the sound of babies crying. The survivors sought the impossible, aching to be put in touch with any form of justice that would stop their terror, and help them cope with their bereavement. In addition communications were very poor.

How difficult was it for Peter Paul to watch his friends being killed?

'You had no feelings. It sounds terrible, but emotionally you were numb. It was over. We fought and lost. Death was inevitable. It was over. You knew you had to die and you just prayed to God that your torture would be short and that you died quickly.'

Did they know at the outset that surrender meant extermination? 'Of course not. We knew that they would want to take revenge on the men and that we would all be killed, but in our worst nightmares we never thought the women and the children would be butchered.'

There is a strong undercurrent of anger in his voice as he describes the way the international community has effectively washed its hands of the Bosnian crisis. Whether or not the country was previously divided along ethnic lines, the effect of the genocide was to confirm a genuine gulf – between those who were the targets of murder and those who did the murdering. Death stalked the roads and ditches. It seemed that the international community was not interested. The little humanitarian aid that was provided was apparently intended to relieve the troubled consciences of the world's television viewers, rather than to provide long-term aid to Bosnia. Peter Paul has a particular reason to feel bitter: 'We got so many promises but no help. All that came was the Prince of Death. The Jews, in particular, were very concerned before we surrendered and wanted to try and escape. They thought the Serbs were like the Nazis. To my shame, I persuaded the sixty of them to stay because I told them that the UN would surely come. I reminded them of how quickly the UN had intervened in Kuwait. They believed me, but no one came and they all died. I can assure you that if you persuaded sixty people, including thirty children and ten women to stay and all were killed you would feel very guilty.'

Has he any hope for the future?

'I would like to think my little god-niece will grow up and maybe marry a nice Serbian boy, and sometime in the future we can put all this madness and hate behind us. It is hard to have hope. Things are very bad.'

As an eyewitness to such horrendous tragedy what does he now believe?

'I believe in justice. To take just one example, we hardly had any hospitals left during the ethnic cleansing. Amputations were often carried out without anaesthetic. Doctors managed because they had to manage. For old people, it was the worst. They came through World War II, but now they see everything they have worked for destroyed. Would you like to see the place you had been born and bred in turned into a giant cemetery?

'Life was not really life for many of them. There was no living just existence. I believe we should all have the chance to live.'

LIVE NUN RUNNING

Sr Helen Prejean

The enduring memory of a meeting with Sr Helen Prejean is that she smiles a lot. Yet the type of work she does is not conducive to laughter. Her gripping autobiographical book, *Dead Man Walking*, was nominated for the Pulitzer Prize and also won the 1994 American Library Association Notable Book of the Year. The acclaimed film director Tim Robbins was so inspired by Helen's book that he adapted it for the screenplay of his movie of the same name, which starred Susan Sarandon in an Oscar winning role. The film has brought Helen and her work to millions around the world.

In 1982, when she was invited to write to a prisoner on Death Row who had brutally killed two teenagers, she had little idea how much it would change her life. Although she abhorred his crime, she befriended the man, Patrick Sonnier, as he faced the electric chair.

'The previous year I had moved to work in a parish in New Orleans. At the time my main concern was to stay alive, as death was rampant – from guns, disease and addiction. Myself and the five other nuns were practically the only whites in the town and poverty and crime were high. The reason for my coming was tied in to what was happening in the Catholic Church at the time, seeking to harness religious faith to social justice. Back in 1971, the worldwide synod of bishops had declared justice a "constitutive" part of the preaching of the Gospel.

'The mandate to tackle social injustice is unsettling because taking on the struggles of the poor invariably means challenging the wealthy and those who serve their interests. In 1980 my religious community, the Sisters of St Joseph of Medaille, had made a commitment to "stand on the side of the poor," and I had assented – but I have to confess only reluctantly.'

The invitation from a member of the Prison Coalition was to write to Patrick Sonnier who was on Death Row for the murder of David LeBlanc, and the rape and murder of Loretta Bourque. Sr Helen would later discover that the rape and murders were committed by Patrick's brother Eddie. Patrick was guilty of collusion. Nonetheless, because of the rigidities of the American legal system, she was unable to get the courts to recognise this fact, with the result that Eddie was allowed to live but Patrick wasn't.

'I had been very naive, because I always thought our system of justice was pretty good. How wrong I was! I think a lot of people are aware of the irregularities of the judicial system since the OJ Simpson case. We have a saying in America that goes "them without the capital get the punishment", because those with the capital are never really punished. It frightens me to think that eighty-two people who were on Death Row have come off because they were shown to be innocent after they were convicted of murder.'

Given the horrific crimes Patrick Sonnier was convicted of, did Sr Helen have any moral qualms about getting involved with him?

'I could not accept that the state planned to kill Patrick in cold blood, but the thought of the young victims haunted me at first. The details of the depravity stunned me. A boy and girl, their young lives budding, were just blown away. In sorting out my feelings and beliefs, there was one piece of moral ground of which I was absolutely certain: if I were to be murdered I would not want my murderer executed. I would not want my death avenged. Especially by a government that can't be trusted to control its own bureaucrats or collect taxes equitably or fill a pothole, much less decide which of its citizens to kill.

'As I corresponded with Pat I began to notice something about him: in each of his letters he expressed gratitude and appreciation for my care and made no demands. He never asked for me. He only said how glad he was to have somebody to communicate with because he was so lonely. The sheer weight of his loneliness, his abandonment, drew me. I abhorred the evil he had done. But I sensed something, some sheer and essential humanness, and that led me to investigate how I could meet him.

'In Matthew: 25, Jesus gave us the test for the way to follow him. "I was hungry and you fed me. I was thirsty and you gave me to drink. I was in prison and you visited me." I had never believed that that passage was meant to apply to me – but all of a sudden it did.'

The problem was that she was not visiting just an ordinary prison, she was going to Death Row – it was a very emotional experience.

'My stomach was in knots. I was there for a two-hour visit and I was very apprehensive until I met Patrick. He was freshly shaven and his black hair was combed into a wave in the front. All of us have been taught to think of people on Death Row as monsters, but this man didn't seem like a monster. He was very lonely because no one was visiting him. His mother had visited him once, but she was never able to go back.'

Sr Helen's emotional toll was much deeper when, after all the legal options had been exhausted, she accompanied Patrick to his death after knowing him for two and a half years.

'They strapped him in the electric chair. A metal cap was placed on his head and an electrode was screwed in at the top and connected to a wire that came from a box behind the chair. He grimaced. He could not speak anymore. A greyish cloth was placed over his face. Then there were three clanks as the switch was pulled with pauses in between. Nineteen hundred volts, then they let the body cool, then five hundred volts, another pause, then nineteen hundred volts. Then the doctor checked him to confirm he was dead.'

If Helen has no misgivings about her involvement with Patrick Sonnier, she does have one regret about one aspect of her early involvement in this ministry.

'The one thing I should have done is to have contacted the victims' families. I didn't think they would want to have anything to do with me because of my campaign to save Patrick, but then I met Lloyd LeBlanc who had lost his son because of the Sonniers. He told me that he would have been very grateful for my support because there was so much pressure on him to advocate the death penalty for Patrick. Many people thought that if he loved his son properly he must push for the death penalty for his murderer.

'He went to Patrick's execution, not for revenge, but hoping for an apology. Before sitting in the electric chair Patrick had said, "Mr LeBlanc, I want to ask your forgiveness for what me and Eddie done," and Lloyd LeBlanc had nodded his head, signifying a forgiveness he had already given. He says that when he arrived with sherrif's duties there in the canefield to identify his son – "laying down there with his two little eyes sticking out like bullets" – he prayed the Our Father. And when he came to the words, "Forgive us our trespasses as we forgive those who trespass against us," he had continued, and he said, "Whoever did this, I forgive them."

'He told me later that, although it was in the middle of the night, after the execution he went straight to his parish priest and asked him to hear his confession and he said, "Father, tonight I've been a witness to something dirty."

'Since Patrick, I have journeyed with four other people to their deaths on Death Row and I am very conscious now of the families of the people they have killed as well as the families of the people executed, because they too become victims.'

As a relentless campaigner against the death penalty, Sr Helen is a frequent visitor to Ireland – on this occasion as a guest of

Lifelines, the organisation that encourages people to become pen-pals of people on Death Row.

'I can't stress enough just how important letters to people on Death Row are. They have no one to visit them in many cases and feel utterly alone and rejected, so just to know that someone from Ireland, or anywhere, is concerned enough about them to take the time and the trouble to write to them means an awful lot to their self-esteem. People are confined to small cells the size of a bathroom and are experiencing sensory deprivation and are completely cut off. So imagine the lift a letter gives them. These letters really are lifelines to people who have nothing else to look forward to.'

Another campaign close to Sr Helen's heart is one designed to mark the new millenium by having a moratorium on the use of the death penalty. She feels that there is an alternative to the 'eye for an eye' mentality.

'The way of Jesus is forgiveness. Forgiveness is never going to be easy. Each day it must be prayed for and struggled for and won.'

A BOATMAN FOR ALL SEASONS

Dick Warner

A soft-spoken, gentle man, Dick Warner was born in 1946 in England, of Anglo-Irish parents. As a child Dick travelled a lot because his father had itchy feet – the family lived, amongst other places, in Addis Ababa and Vienna – he got very little formal secondary education. Returning to Ireland in the early sixties, he attended school briefly in Belfast and went to Trinity College Dublin.

'In 1965 I walked through the front gate of Trinity College as a nineteen-year-old undergraduate wearing a sports jacket and grey flannel trousers with turn-ups, a short-back-and-sides and a bald chin. The twenty-three-year-old who walked through that gate in 1969 with a Second Class Honours Degree was a very different person. He had shoulder-length hair and a beard and wore a long black cloak over knee-length black leather boots. He had stood with a group outside the American Embassy getting their pictures taken by CIA agents as they chanted "Hey, Hey, LBJ – How many kids you kill today?" His most important baggage was a collection of ideas and values that were to last into the third millennium. He was almost completely a sixties product. Looking back, my main impression of the sixties is of a narrow beam of light that illuminated the century between the greyness of post-war austerity and the greyness of post-oil-crisis recession.'

After Trinity the travelling started again, with a spell in Germany, frequent periods in the United States and a time in England, before he returned to Ireland. In the seventies, he joined RTÉ as a radio producer and, for a while, lived on a boat moored in the Grand Canal. What attracted him to a career in radio?

'I was fortunate enough to leave college at a time when the question was not whether or not you would get a job but whether you would get one that paid £1000 per year or not – that was big money in those days. At college, I had been involved in student journalism and was very interested in a career as a writer using the broadest possible definition, which incorporated broadcasting. It is a very intellectually stimulating environment, especially for someone like me who has something of a short concentration span, because there is such variety in the job. Another advantage of radio, as distinct from television, is that you have a lot of creative control. It's also given me a great opportunity to travel to interesting places. I think I can safely say I'm one of the few Irish broadcasters who, whilst making a Christmas programme about reindeers, has been involved in a reindeer accident in Lapland!'

One of his most vivid memories of his radio programmes was of making a radio documentary on Mother Teresa.

'Jim Fahy and I went to Calcutta for five days to make the programme in the late 1970s. It was before she had won the Nobel Peace Prize and she didn't have the profile then that she has now. We lived in her convent and basically we followed her around on her daily routine beginning with Mass at 5 a.m. right through until 8p.m. I'm not sure if she maintained that same pace, but at that time this frail, blue-eyed Albanian peasant woman had incredible energy. She had so many houses and places to visit: homes for the dying and destitute, a leper colony and so on. To my eyes, she was a saint or almost a saint. It's pretty awe-inspiring, not just to meet someone like that, but to share her company for a reasonably lengthy period of time. Her conviction was absolute. I've never met anybody who allowed themselves less time for questioning. She had this wall of certainty about what her calling was. My enduring memory, though, is of her charity.'

Is he a religious or spiritual person himself?

'My grandfather was a Church of Ireland rector. My father is a communist atheist, so I never had anything to rebel against! I'm a cultural Protestant. If we accept the distinction between organised religion and spirituality that your question implies then I would describe myself as a spiritual person in that I have strong spiritual feelings about my love of nature. It's tied up with a love of life, especially with the evolutionary energy of life. Much of nature, like a polar ice-cap, can be very thrilling in purely aesthetic terms, but it's the life-generating aspect of creation that fascinates me. I visited the Sahara Desert, which was an incredibly interesting experience, but it was the footprints in the sand dunes that most appealed to me. I've always read a lot. One of the most formative influences on my spiritual values has been the writing of Charles Darwin, especially his attitudes to life.'

As if to prove the point of his commitment to nature, he currently lives on a small-holding in County Kildare with his wife Geraldine, two sons Luke and Sam, three cats, a dog, nine hens and a cock and three sheep. He is a very independent thinker and finds any kind of dogmatism, religious or otherwise unpalatable.

A famous story is told about St Francis of Assisi. One day two young men came to Francis, saying that they wanted to join his friars. Francis looked at them and said, 'Before accepting you, I would like you to do something for me.' As he said this, he stooped down, picked up two cabbage plants and handed one to each of the two men. Pointing to a small patch of newly-dug soil, he asked them to plant the cabbages. They were about to do this, when Francis added, 'There is just one more thing. I want you to plant them outside down, with the leaves buried and the roots in the air.' Immediately, one of the men picked up a trowel and did what

Francis directed. The other politely pointed out that if the cabbages were planted like that they would never grow. This prospective monk was asked to return home while the first man was enthusiastically welcomed into the brotherhood. This type of blind obedience is anathema to Dick Warner.

In the mid-eighties Warner received a potentially devasting blow when he was diagnosed as having Multiple Sclerosis.

'MS cannot be diagnosed on one set of symptoms. I was having pins and needles and problems with my eyesight and went to my doctor. Having being in a leper colony when I went to India, I read a book on leprosy and because of the similar symptoms I convinced myself that I had leprosy. When I told this to the doctor he nearly fell off his chair laughing! It's not possible to acquire the condition in the way I had envisaged.'

Faced with a crisis, our emotions and thoughts can surprise, even shock by their depth, variety and complexity. The Beruit hostage Brian Keenan describes his dark moments during his imprisonment as those of 'a man hanging by his fingernails over the edge of chaos feeling his fingers slowly straightening.' This also serves as an apt summary of the darkest chapter of Warner's life and the sense of utter despair and fear.

'The initial couple of years after the diagnosis were extremely traumatic psychologically. It's the vagueness that creates the stress. In some ways it is almost better to be told you have got six months to live. The advice I would give to someone who gets a diagnosis of MS, or to their friends, is never to underestimate the psychological trauma.

'My symptoms haven't developed in the last ten years, so it would appear that I have a benign form of the disease. The prognosis is much better now. It's a disease that chiefly attacks young people, which is another plus point in my favour.'

News of his illness spurred him on to achieve some of the ambitions he had been thinking about.

'MS, like hanging, concentrates the mind beautifully. I had been putting things on the long finger, but with MS I knew that the finger wasn't long enough any more.'

One particular aspiration he had nurtured was to present television programmes. The result was four series of the internationally acclaimed, award-winning *Waterways* television documentaries. Apart from his television work he writes books and articles and gives lectures on environmental topics.

In Chinese, the word 'crisis' is composed of two characters. One represents danger and the other opportunity. Dick Warner turns difficulties into opportunities and his life is a testimony to the power of positive thinking.

FATHER FORGIVE THEM

Gordon Wilson

'Where were you the night John F. Kennedy was shot?' This was a question I had often heard posed as I was growing up, but I never really understood the power of a single event to remain frozen in the memory until Remembrance Sunday, 1987. Even the hardest heart could not but have been touched by Gordon Wilson's intensely moving account of how he lay bleeding under the rubble, clutching his daughter's hand and heard her fading voice saying: 'Daddy, I love you very much.' Immediately after the carnage caused by an IRA bomb, as part of their ongoing struggle to end British occupation in Ireland, communal passions threatened to explode. In this highly charged atmosphere, Gordon's words of forgiveness defused an extremely volatile situation.

I met him in Enniskillen less than a year after the death of his daughter. We talked about Marie, the child who was sired by so many dreams and by so much love. He untangled from the sea of dogma a simple message that true religion is about love not hate – about reaching out in handshake and not with clenched fists.

'When I spoke that day I was only speaking for myself. I never envisaged that my words would have the impact they did. If I had time to reflect I would have wanted to be more eloquent but I think people seemed to respond better to sincerity than eloquence. Maybe there is an important lesson for us there.'

In his reaction to his daughter Marie's murder, Gordon Wilson alerted us to the fact that forgiveness and excusing are not simply different but polar opposites. If one was not really to blame, then there is nothing to forgive. To excuse somebody who can really produce good excuses is not Christian charity; it is only fairness. To be a Christian means to forgive the inexcusable, because God has forgiven the inexcusable in us. Even on the cross Jesus was offering words of forgiveness to the people who were trying to kill him in the most cruel and degrading way imaginable. With almost his dying breath he whispered a prayer of forgiveness. Only forgiveness can achieve this. It is only through forgiveness that we are set free for freedom.

Throughout our history the abuse of religion has brought nothing but division to our troubled country. When Gordon Wilson forgave the inexcusable he showed that Christianity is a potentially healing and unifying force in our society. In his darkest hour, his words of forgiveness showed that the gentleness of Christianity is stronger than a terrorist's bomb.

'Every father thinks that their own daughter is sweeter than everyone else's. I suppose I was no different. I think, though, she was a very good person. I know that sounds very pious and that kind of language is not fashionable today. I didn't want to contaminate Marie's memory by using dirty talk. Nothing that I could say was going to bring Marie back. I couldn't bring myself to wish hate on the people who killed my daughter. Not everybody understood. I am sad to report that I lost friends beause of what I said that day but I did what I thought was right and I am prepared to accept the consequences.

'To be honest, I am still shocked about the fuss I created. All I tried to do was to do what Jesus asked. As he hung on the cross: what did he say? "Father forgive them they know not what they do." If you are a Christian you have to at least try and live your life as Jesus asked. I'm not saying that is always easy. In fact a lot of the time it is really hard.'

Meeting Gordon Wilson, I was reminded of George Eliot's *Daniel Deronda* where Gwendolen Harleth married the revolting Grandcourt in order to provide money for her family. She hoped she would dominate him with the strength of her personality, but when she was unsuccessful she came to hate him. One day she was sailing in a small boat with him, and she was harbouring murderous thoughts against him; he was swept overboard and though she tried to save him, he was drowned. He died while she was wishing death on him, so she felt that she was in a sense an accomplice to murder. She carries a deep sense of guilt around with her and feels she can never be forgiven, which takes her to Deronda for guidance.

Deronda does not attempt to tell her she is wrong to condemn herself; he does not seek to take her pain away from her; he does not try to replace her flood of grief and accusation with soothing cliches of comfort. It would not be in Gwendolen's interests to fail to take seriously the wrong she feels she has been guilty of. However, he is aware that in the hour of darkness she has come, for the first time, to that point of self-knowledge about the worst side of her nature and that she will not grow unless she is allowed to have that pain of knowledge.

While she did not cause her husband's death, it was accompanied by her own murderous thoughts. Hers is, to use the traditional term, a sin of the heart. Neither event can be undone: her husband will remain dead, and she cannot change what she felt towards him, but from Deronda's perspective, these terrible events can alter other things, how she lives the rest of her life. Deronda initiates the process of healing by taking the struggle within Gwendolen seriously as, for the first time, she is confronted with the truth of her nature. The tyranny of the past can be broken; the sin of the past can be healed in the future – not by minimising the seriousness of the past, but by putting the past in the perspective of a different future.

No one understood this better than Gordon Wilson. He was a man who dedicated his final years to breaking free of the tyranny of the past and trying to put his own troubled past in the perspective of a better future for our troubled island.

Despite the trauma of the Enniskillen bombing, Gordon Wilson never lost his seeds of faith or hope. On the contrary, those virtues blossomed in adversity. Out of the darkness came light. Touching rock bottom he abandoned himself to reach out to the transcendent. Having entered a new world of suffering and fear, without any familiar landmarks, in his vulnerability and powerlessness Gordon experienced total dependence on God. This was not an academic exercise but an authentic human Calvary. Yet Gordon saw in the darkness, physical and emotional, of his condition that God was with him in a very real way, transforming the savage into the sacred. The physical legacy of the day of the explosion was most evident in the awkward way he tried to light a cigarette. The bomb blast left him with greatly diminished power in one hand. He fought manfully to disguise his annoyance with his incapacity.

'When you think of my physical sufferings from the bomb, I got away very light. I can cope with it easy enough – it is much more difficult to cope with Marie's loss.'

Through all his suffering Gordon felt a deep sense of being held in the loving embrace of God, an experience that brought him great consolation. Surrendering wholeheartedly to God, Gordon contemplated Jesus on the cross, and came to a new understanding of the depth of the mystery of God's love for us. He rejoiced in the Lord in spite of, indeed because of, all the sufferings human life is heir to. The joy and gratitude that marked his courage seemed strangely alien in the light of his pain at the time.

Suffering often appears to be an unanswerable conundrum for those who believe in the Christian God and it often rouses us to anger. Yet Gordon Wilson believed that God was present in his suffering, hanging on the cross of contradiction, and that new life could flow from the dark mystery of the Enniskillen bombing.

'Have no doubts, I had many a dark day since Marie died, but whenever I was at my lowest God sent me something to get me through it. People think I was very strong. I wasn't. I simply surrendered to God.'

Gordon Wilson is a living symbol of all that is best in our shared heritage. Symbols give us our identity, self-image, our way of explaining ourselves to ourselves and to others. In the Christian tradition the cross is the ultimate symbol. Today this cross remains as a poignant, and appropriate, reminder of a man who embodied the Christian virtue of loving without counting the cost and who tragically paid the ultimate price. Through this cross a man long dead lives again, somehow speaking to his people down through the years.

My abiding memory of Gordon Wilson, though, is of an incident the day we met. As we spoke above his draper's shop in Enniskillen his two young grandchildren burst in the door. His serious face broke into the most magnificent warm smile and his eyes lit up when he saw them. To many people this soft-spoken native of County Leitrim will always be remembered as a man who embodied the Christian virtue of forgiveness. I remember him though, as I remember my own grandfather, as a man who doted on his grandchildren.

'I believe that for the sake of our children and our grandchildren we can't stay trapped in the past. For too long we have been like prisoners in cells. We must break free and end the "them and us" mentality. We've got to change our attitudes and our mindsets. People have to understand that it is not about negotiating convictions but about walking a path together.'

THE WHISPERING BREEZE

Marion Carroll

On a drab and uninspiring evening in August 1879, a small community witnessed the apparition of Our Lady at Knock through sheets of driving rain and howling wind. The visitation gave hope to a famine-stricken, persecuted region. Today, pilgrims continue to flock to Knock. The real miracle of Knock is that the black clouds are lifted – at least temporarily. The most frequent healing is on the inside.

In 1989, after seventeen years of debilitating illness, Marion Carroll was a human wreck. She could not walk; her muscles were wasted; she was blind in one eye and had only partial sight in the other. She had lost control of her bladder; the muscles of her throat were damaged and her speech was severely affected; and she had a hiatus hernia, thyroid trouble and epilepsy. That September, against all medical advice, Marion attended the Anointing of the Sick in the Basilica of the shrine of Knock.

'The knowledge that I could have died, that I had to assess my performance in life, produced a very real desire in me to live, if God willed it. I felt that I still had something to contribute to my family. I think that my own particular religious faith, which is strongly grounded in the love of God and the Holy Family and in the hope that springs from this, kept me going. I felt that the Holy Family has been a guiding hand and, in that way, my general attitude, and approach to what should be done was much better attuned to dealing with priorities.

'One of the benefits of the illness to me has been that it has intensified this personal relationship to a remarkable extent. Until then, God tended to be somebody remote to whom I gave orthodox prayer and to whom I paid homage at Mass. As I talked to God during my illness in a more personal way, I began to develop an even more intimate relationship with Him.

'I often think that it must be very difficult to achieve peace without prayer. Prayer was my great buttress during my illness because from prayer I got hope and confidence. This is enormously important when you are lying on your bed all day because it gives you the right psychological attitude to a serious illness. There are two sides to it; the practical and the spiritual. But it all stems from a resurrection of the human spirit fortified by belief in the love of God.

'The Bible tells us: "I can do all things in Christ who strengthens me." I believe that the truth these affirmations express is powerful for one's self-confidence and that it can pull you out of the depths of difficulty and despair. In the words of St Paul: "He who believes in God can surmount any heights or depths." To believe in the power of God is, in my view, a very important anchor to have, because it enables one to survive in times of tribulation and to fight against the very real difficulties that would otherwise cause one to despair.

'While I never totally despaired, I was close to it on many occasions. Then when I went back to be fortified by the Holy Family, the confidence that this gave me helped me to feel that nobody could be against me or beat me if He was on my side. I believed that God was on my side and this was a tremendous source of strength during all of my serious illness.

'I think that my illness also helped me to focus my attention on my relationships. I think I was always people orientated in terms of getting on with people. But certainly it helped heighten my perception of and gave greater meaning to my relationships, particularly with my husband and family. The enormous sustenance that they were to me during that particular period had a great impact on our relationship as a family. It has helped in my relations with people in general.'

The two poles of Marion's emotional state at this time are evident in every sentence as she recalls those months; the scream and the whisper, the tumultuous and the gentle, the loud exhortation and the protective veil – arising from her own inner turmoil and her love for the family:

'I feel that my whole human spirit needed to be lifted and I don't think I could have lifted it on my own. Having the Lord with me was an enormous help in taking me away from the brink of despair. At all times I prayed that whatever His will decreed, I would offer myself on that basis. And if it would be His will that I survive, well then I would do my best to justify that decision on His part.

'Yet there were times when my faith flagged. It is not easy to always look on the bright side of life when you know you are dying. A local chaplain had even begun to write the homily for my funeral.'

The Gospels are full of Good News – God's love for us, hope, life, wisdom and truth. Marion discovered a great happiness and peace within herself because God was there patiently waiting with open arms for her. It was the type of feeling described by Job: 'In the past, I knew only what others had told me, but now I have seen you with my own eyes'(Job 42:5). God was the silence, a voice that spoke without words, a quiet that is loud with conviction, the calm at the centre of a storm.

It was also good to know that others could help her somehow by praying for her body and soul. This was a bed-rock Catholic tradition, based on an unshakable belief in the mercy of God, a belief that predated Christianity and received its first expression in Judas Maccabeus.

Surprisingly, given Marion's few opportunities for any kind of social outlet, she was not all that keen to travel to Knock when the opportunity arose:

'When Gerry Glynn of the Order of Malta in Athlone asked me would I go to Knock I said I would go anywhere to get away from the four walls. It didn't mean too much to me. I thought it was cold and barren. The last time I was there it was lashing rain and there was a gale blowing. That day too we found trouble getting a wheelchair. I thought it was the most miserable place and we got in the car and went home.'

On that September day, though, things would turn out to be very different.

'When the ceremonies started, my bishop walked down with the Eucharist during the blessing of the sick and came to the front of my stretcher, I heard the words, "The lame shall walk". When the ceremonies started, my bishop anointed me. After Communion I got this magnificent feeling – a wonderful sensation – like a whispering breeze telling me that I was cured. I got this magnificent, beautiful feeling telling me that if the stretcher was opened I could get up and walk.'

When Mass was over, she stepped, free from pain, from her stretcher and walked.

'In the first few months after my cure I kept asking myself: why me, why was I chosen to be cured? The answer came while saying the family rosary six months later. That gift was not to me alone, but to the people of the world, to let them know that God was there, and that all people had to do was to ask and they would receive. People tell me prayer has not worked for them, but just as we are very good at telling our children what is best for them, God knows what is best for us.

'A few months after my cure I said to my husband, Jimmy, that the family would go to Medjugore, before the year was out. He just laughed out loud and asked: "On what. Fresh air or hot water?" Although we could not afford to even think about it, somebody paid anonymously for us to go there. We were thrilled! But during Mass there, I had a very unusual experience. My hands seemed to have a life of their own and were opening out wide. Around each hand there was a beautiful glow of light. I feared I was hallucinating.

'The glow was the glow of love. It looked like there was a single heart in the palm of each hand. They stayed like that for the rest of Mass. It was as if my hand were in the Lord's hands. There was just one pulse – the pulse that is the love in his heart for people. I turned to Our Lady's altar and said the Hail Mary.

'After Mass I had a desire to go to confession and the priest said to me: "Would you lay your hands on me and pray with me? You have been given a very special gift from God." All I could say was: "May the Lord help me, because I knew nothing about this." During that whole trip my cup of happiness was overflowing, although it took me a year to figure out all that happened. I know now that God was telling me that my cure was not for myself, but so that I could go and spread the news of God's love and healing to others.'

Having returned home from her trip, Marion went to her bishop and asked his permission to speak from the altar at her local church. She now gives healing ministries at various churches throughout Ireland.

She asks the same questions, wrestles with the same problems and faces the same pain and anguish as her audience. She too has confronted the loneliness and despair that so many people suffer from in Ireland today. Her faith and love has not shielded her from pain and anguish.

'Self-pity has no place in my life. I will never accept that I was the victim of Multiple Sclerosis. Jimmy was. After Knock there were no more victims in our family. I want to let people know that when they are suffering, they are not alone.'

GO PLACIDLY AMID THE NOISE AND HASTE

Tony Ward

Fame is a vapour, popularity is an accident; the only earthly certainty is oblivion.

Mark Twain

No Irish sportstar, apart from George Best, has filled more newspaper columns than Tony Ward. This is best illustrated by an example. During his time as national rugby coach, Mick Doyle was guest speaker at a luncheon of the Irish Business Association in the London Metropole Hotel, and was quoted as attacking newspaper reporting of rugby as 'insensitive', 'wildly inaccurate' and 'pseudo-aggressive'. He made particular reference to the harsh treatment given by newspaper reporters to the Irish selectors because of their failure to pick Tony Ward. As an example of the distortions in the print media he told the 'parable' of an Irishman who fell under a tube train in London and was killed. The *London Times* reported it straight, the *Sun* that an Irish terrorist had disrupted British Rail schedules, the *Irish Independent* that a Scotsman had been killed at Heathrow, the *Irish Press* that British Rail had murdered an innocent Irishman and the *Irish Times* that Tony Ward had his travel schedule disrupted because of a mishap on British Rail.

Ward exploded onto the sporting scene in 1978 when he first played for Ireland. Already he was a local hero in Limerick – where he was training to be a PE teacher in Thomond College – because of his displays for one of the city's top teams, Garryowen.

'When I accepted an invitation to play for Garryowen it was to change my life. I knew that rugby meant a lot to the people of Limerick, but it was not until I had direct involvement that I realised just how much it meant. The game is a way of life in Limerick.'

As his fame spread there was speculation that he would return to Dublin to play for his alma mater, St Mary's College. Ward was the unnamed culprit in a story that did the rounds just as he broke onto the Irish team. The story involved two conversations between a Young Munster (Garryowen's great rivals) supporter and his parish priest.

Priest: 'Tis a long time since your face has been seen in this sacred house my son. Anyway we cater for all types here. Can I be of any assistance to you at all?'

Fan: 'I don't know if you can Father. You see this could be a job for the bishop. I am in an awful way. My state of mind is such that all communications with the wife, both verbal and otherwise, have temporarily ceased.'

Priest: 'My son, confession is good for the soul. What is the terrible secret that you bear?'

Fan: 'Father, the truth is . . . I . . . I . . . am in danger of becoming a supporter of the Garryowen team.'

Priest: 'I see. That's bad, in fact, it's very bad.'

Fan: 'I knew you would understand, Father. All my life I thought that rugby consisted of rucks, scrums and line-outs with a few fights thrown in for good measure. Where I come from, shouts of "ahead, ahead" have a different meaning than those employed elsewhere. To be candid, Father, I was happy in my ignorance, but now tis all jinking and running, reverse-passing and blind-side moves. And to make matters worse, father, I am being entertained by it all. Tell me . . . Do you think I could be losing the faith?'

Priest: 'My son, the ordinary, everyday problems of life – wife-swopping, divorce, drinking – are but minor problems compared to your dilemma. Come back to me tomorrow, I shall have spoken with a higher authority by then.'

The next day:

Priest: 'My son you can put your mind to rest. A solution to your problem exists and where else was it to be found but in . . . religion. Within a year or two the blackguard most responsible for Garryowen's madness and for your unhappy state of mind will be plucked from our midst and transported away. Normality will return.'

Fan: 'But how can I be sure of this?'

Priest: 'My son, the bells of St Mary's will ring out for him . . . and he will answer their call.'

Given his outstanding displays for Ireland in 1978 and 1979 and his pivotal role in Munster's historic victory over the All-Blacks in 1978, Ward was voted European Player of the Year in both seasons. Then when his career was at its height he was sensationally dropped from the Irish team on tour in Australia in 1979, in favour of Ollie Campbell.

When Shakespeare wrote, 'There is a tide in the affairs of men', he could not have foreseen events in Irish rugby a few hundred years later. Ward's tide came in on the Australian tour in 1979 and much of his life in rugby and outside sport was shaped, and to some extent, remains defined by that experience. Years on from those heady days Ward is still to a certain degree, despite his best efforts to the contrary, wearing the invisible scars from that experience.

Although he is no 'holy Joe', religion was a great support to him in his time of need.

'I was a long way from home and I was really down and lonely and I think it's at times like that you find God. I've said this to Brian D'arcy a few times, because Brian has been a good friend down through the years, "Surely when you are down, or have a problem, or need something it is wrong to turn to God", but Brian said no, because that is why God is there. I think, as long as you can carry on your life in the proper way, God is there as a friend and I don't think with that philosophy you can go far wrong.'

Ward's friendship with Fr Brian has brought its memorable moments.

'I called out to meet Brian in Mount Argus in 1989. It was the feast of St Blaise and there were hundreds of people at Mass having their throats blessed and afterwards I went to meet Fr Brian in the dining hall for a cuppa. There were two other men there. One I knew well – Joe Dolan. The other I genuinely didn't know from Adam. However, his star has certainly risen a lot since . . . It was Daniel O'Donnell!'

Ward experienced crises in his new career as a businessman as well as in rugby. He was forced to close his sports shops – one in Cathedral Street, off O'Connell Street in Dublin, and the other in Dún Laoghaire.

'We were hit by the recession. It was as simple as that and as a result we were forced into voluntary liquidation. We tried to keep the lease open, but in the end the heartbreaking decision had to be made.'

Since his retirement from rugby in 1988, Ward has drawn on his experience as a player at the highest level to become a match analyst and rugby journalist. He has the ability to highlight technical aspects of play that might go unnoticed to the casual observer, as well as the self-confidence to articulate his views honestly and in a forthright manner.

He has also been heavily involved in coaching. Although Ward has never been one for thumping fists on tables, he makes his point forcibly:

'I think there is so much pressure now to win that the enjoyment is going out of rugby and that shouldn't happen, because rugby is still a sport and a leisure activity. As a PE teacher, my job was to offer as many sports as possible and schools are increasingly providing more sports for children. I felt that if they left school and chose to play one sport afterwards I had succeeded as a teacher.

'One philosophy I have is that I never, ever transmit negative comments to kids on the field. The day that I do that is the day that I hang up my coaching boots, so to speak. Certainly a few days later I will point out the mistakes that were made on the training field. No player goes on to the field deliberately trying to make a mistake, and I do get very annoyed when I hear teammates chastising a player on the field or, worse still, a coach shouting abuse at a kid from the sideline.'

While Ward retains his enthusiasm for rugby, it is when he talks about his wife and family that he really becomes animated. Until he reaches this part of his story, his eyes have been glazed with the pain of reliving the trauma of the Australian experience for the millionth time: when we reach the part about Louise he lights up like a Christmas tree.

'When Louise came into my life she completely bowled me over. I had no idea I could be consumed with so much love for someone. Louise gives me the love, security and strength that I didn't believe possible. The highlights of my life, apart from her, are my four children. I'm a lucky man that Louise came into my life.'

If every man is a king of his own castle, then the court of King Tony is in a quiet, southside suburb, with plenty of greenery and little traffic. The immediate impression is of a good place to bring up kids. The greeting is hardly regal, though always warm and genuine.

One of the many striking things about a visit to Ward's home is his apparent fondness for the old song 'Desiderata'.

'I am a child of the sixties. When I look back on the time, I'm struck by the innocence of it all. The songs were so meaningful remember Dylan, and Simon and Garfunkel? There was an idealism that just isn't there today.

'I'm delighted to have lived then, to have been young in a time when there wasn't a serious drug or alcohol problem, when the word AIDS had never been heard of.

'Luxembourg was the only station when I was growing up. I remember doing my homework listening to it, and they used to have this power play, every hour, on the hour. I remember one year there was a Les Crane song called 'Desiderata' that was in the form of a prayer. To this day, I have the words of that prayer hung up in three different places in my house. I'm sure everybody has heard it even if they don't recognize the title. It is the one that begins: 'Go placidly amid the noise and haste. . .

'There's a line in 'Desiderata': "Be at peace with your God, whatever or whoever you believe him to be". I'm at peace with my conscience, I'm at peace with my mind and I'm at peace with my maker. At the end of the day, what it's all about is that when you are called to meet your maker you can look into your soul and say you did it the right way, and more than that I don't know.'

ALL IN THE GAME

Mick Byrne and Jack Charlton

In the glory days of Jack Charlton's reign as Irish soccer manager, one of the best known faces on Irish television was the team's physio, Mick Byrne. Mick is the archetypal Dub.

'I was born and raised in the inner city, in City Quay. My two aunties, Lord have mercy on them, worked in the chapel, so I was very attached to it from a very early age. I used to help them clean the church, cut the grass for the priest and I went in for meals with them. My favourite thing of all was to ring the Angelus bell.

'Religion, at the time, was everything. You were always scared of it back then. Looking back now there were no reasons for it, but you were always threatened with being brought to the priest if you did anything wrong. Nothing happened of course. I also used to go to the sodalities.'

Listening to Mick Byrne talk about his early years is like turning back the clock to an Ireland that has virtually disappeared. This is most evident listening to his recollections of the missions. The announcement of the mission was greeted with some excitement in the parish. It became a close second to the weather as the most important topic of conversation. The priest tried to drum up some enthusiasm and spiritual fervour by describing it as 'an occasion of grace'. Public enemy number one was sin.

The preparation beforehand was a fastidious enterprise. The trappings and ceremonials of services were more elaborate and formal than usual and all the component parts were done with enormous care for detail. Even the choir's attention to musical offerings of praise was better than usual.

Nevertheless, for most people the mission was really a social event. This sharing of gossip and humour helped to keep the community alive, but also revealed the heartache and quiet desperation that underlined so many lives in the parish.

The sermons went on and on. Now and again a crying or crawling child gave a bit of diversion to the rustling and waiting congregation.

'I was an altar boy, but we were banished from the altar during the missions while the priest was giving his sermon in case we heard anything we shouldn't.'

Another important event at the time included the Stations of the Cross, at six o'clock on a Friday evening. Three altar boys journeyed with the priest as he walked solemnly to each of the stations, two carried candles, and one a big wooden cross. Then the priest forcefully boomed out the chant at each station:

O Jesus for love of me didst bear thy cross to Calvary
In thy sweet mercy grant me to suffer and to die with thee.

Those lines did give a sense of the debt all Christians owed to the Saviour.

Although many of the religious practices of Mick Byrne's childhood are no longer fashionable, he retains a deep love for one key element of Christian liturgy.

'I would really walk miles to get Mass on a Sunday. I have this thing that, whatever country I am in, and I have been to a lot of them with the Irish soccer team, I would get Mass or make sure that Mass is said. One phrase that always stuck in my mind was

something that my mother always said, "The devil loves a Mass misser." This will always be a part of me and I will never give it up.

'I love going to Mass. I don't portray myself as a religious freak because I was always my own man, but I know the importance of looking for religion and of looking for guidance from God. I pray to God and the Blessed Virgin and St Anthony – who is my saint. Any problems I've ever had I always pray to St Anthony.

'There were crossroads in my life and I brought them to God to help me find the right path. I've had to make difficult decisions so I prayed for guidance and those decisions were always right.'

Yet Mick's prayers are never for purely selfish reasons.

'I pray for my children, that they are successful in their work, in their study. One of my girls is away in Tenerife working as a teacher and I pray for her every day, that everything will go well for her, that she'll be healthy and that she'll be happy and the same for my other children and my two grandchildren. Everybody is included in my prayers that things will go right for them – if it's God's will and only if it's God's will.

'I always believe that – even though it may not seem right and I mightn't get the things that I am looking for – it's his will. Likewise if he wants me to have it I will get it because it is God's will.

'It's not easy to do at times, especially in times of sickness and death. I'm very much thinking now of when my mother and sister died. God was very much me with me at those times, in my hours of need.

'I try and block that part out of my mind, which some people tell me is wrong. I haven't gone to see my mother's grave since she died because I can't bear to think of her dead. The same with my sister. They died within a few months of each other and that was a terrible time in my life.

'It's strange, I am really uncomfortable when I think of them dead but I have absolutely no fear of dying myself. I'm ready when he calls me – any time. Mind you, I hope it won't be for a few years yet!'

Mick has a treasure trove of stories about his association with the Irish soccer team, particularly of the glory days with Jack Charlton. He struck up an immediate and enduring friendship with Jack. His face lights up when he talks about soccer. Yet it is perhaps a very revealing insight into his character that the most emotion comes when he recalls the most difficult moment for him in the Charlton era. The incident involved Gary Waddock – the man at the centre of one of the most controversial episodes in Irish soccer. In 1990, at the last moment in the training camp in Malta, Jack Charlton created a sensation by calling up Alan McLoughlin and dropping Waddock from the World Cup squad for Italy. The circumstances of Waddock's exclusion were terribly traumatic for him.

'Waddo' had emerged in the eighties as a tough-tackling and inspirational midfield general with both QPR and Ireland. Then things went horribly wrong for this genial and effervescent Cockney. After a knee injury in 1985, when he ruptured the ligaments in his knee, he was forced to retire. He only ever wanted to be a professional footballer and it came as a big blow to hear that the injury was so bad he had to turn his back on his dreams.

For every good player who has made a successful comeback there are many more who have fallen flat on their face. The revival in Waddock's fortunes was neither swift nor painless. At the behest of QPR he agreed to settle with the insurance company and turn his back on football. Rehabilitation came via a sojourn in Belgium. In his two years in Belgium he never gave up hope that he could get back to the big time in English football.

A bizarre chain of events brought him right back to the upper echelons of the football world. In 1989 he bumped into Jack Charlton at a dinner and he invited him over to join the Irish squad for a testimonial game. He played and it seemed to go well. Tony Cascarino spoke to the then manager at Millwall, John Docherty, about him, and he joined Millwall for two years. Shortly after, he was recalled to the Irish squad and played in a couple of friendly matches in the warm-up for the World Cup in Italy. When he injured his knee his two aims were to get back into the first division and then play with Ireland. When he was called back into the Irish side, after being on the scrapheap, he couldn't believe it

Life could hardly have been sweeter for the born-again international as he flew off with the Irish squad for the World Cup and his date with soccer's elite. Little did he know that his world would quickly collapse on his shoulders.

One minute he was in the World Cup party and the next minute he was out of the squad and getting the plane home. He was devastated. Jack just pulled him aside and said he wasn't going to be included in the twenty-two. It was as simple as that. He told him he could be the twenty-third man, but that was no good to Gary. It was very difficult for him but his disappointment was almost as keenly felt by Mick Byrne. The sadness in his voice and in his eyes as he relates the story says more about Byrne than mere words could ever do.

One of the consequences of the trip to Rome was the opportunity to meet the Pope – an experience that Mick will treasure forever. Jack Charlton explained the significance of the meeting to me.

'I have to say it was a slightly tense occasion for me. I am not a Catholic so I found the ceremonial aspect a bit of a puzzle. We always had a priest in to say Mass for the Irish team and I attended then, but an event with the Pope is something completely different and a very big deal. I didn't know when to go forward and when to go back so I didn't want to embarrass myself or anybody else by making a cock-up. I knew it was a very proud moment for the players and all the staff. For some of them it would be the icing on the cake of probably the biggest event of their football lives, but for others it would be the biggest event of their lives.

'No matter what your religion is, the Vatican is a mighty organisation. The Pope is a very charismatic man, if I can use the word. He is someone that you would like to meet regardless of your own beliefs. He said to me: "Ah, Mr Charlton. The boss." It was nice to bring a Catholic team to see the Pope. I have pictures at home showing me meeting him. I am very happy with those photos.'

How conscious was he of being a manager of a Catholic team when he was in charge of Ireland?

'Well, I never saw anybody kneeling down to say prayers before a match, but they all would have made a sign of the Cross before going out on the pitch. That's natural if you are a Catholic I should think.'

Did Big Jack ever say a prayer before a match himself?

'No, I have never prayed about football, as far as I can remember. I do think it is good to pray though. When my kids were small I got them to say prayers before they went to bed. I remember one time when I was putting my daughter to bed saying: "Kneel down and say your prayers." She said: "Can I say the one we learned in school?" I said: "Course you can". So she knelt down and said: "For what we are about to receive O Lord make us truly grateful." I thought that it was very funny, because it a prayer you say before eating your food. But she was very young then and didn't know any better.'

I was afraid he would choke with laughter when I suggested that he would be canonised by the Irish people because of the success he has achieved with the team.

'Public attention is part of the job. I'm a miner's son from the North East of England who spent a life in football. They gave me a job to do over here, which was to produce a team that would get results and bring people into the game. I've been very successful in doing exactly that. The fact that the people of Ireland like me is great. I like being popular. I would be a liar if I said I didn't. It's got its drawbacks. There is very little privacy anymore. Canonisation? You couldn't have that done to me anyway. I'm a Protestant!'

Although the Charlton era is gone forever, Mick Byrne remains an integral part of the Irish backroom set-up. He is unsure where his adventures with the Irish team will lead him, but there is one certainty in Mick's life.

'I'm very proud to be an Irish Catholic and I will remain so to my dying day.'

MAKING A DIFFERENCE

Suzanne O'Connell

Some people are born to make a difference. Suzanne O'Connell is such a woman. Last summer, Suzanne was one of the medical students from Trinity College's Health Sciences Faculty who spent the summer in a girls' orphanage in Hincesti, Moldova, as part of her training as a doctor. It was an experience that changed her life.

'What we saw and experienced was truly appalling: two hundred girls, from the age of four up to adulthood, with inadequate supervision and no facilities or activities to stimulate them. They had little clothing and no underwear or shoes. Most of the girls had severe physical and neurological disabilities. We saw severe malnutrition, intentional starvation, chronic infectious disease; no medical aid of any significance and little humanitarian aid; deficient medical care of the children and vital medications withheld from them; mismanagement of drugs supplied to the orphanage. We were aware of sexual abuse and found that some of the children were forced into prostitution. In addition, the temperatures are more than forty degrees in summer and below minus thirty in winter.

'When we came home we decided to set up an organisation to provide help for these girls. It is called OutReach Moldova. Unfortunately there are seventy-one such orphanages in the country, with forty-six thousand children; this is a country that is just five hours away by plane and the poorest in Europe. Wonderful volunteers from Trinity, Cork, Dublin and the North of Ireland have joined me. I have taken a year out of my studies to put OutReach Moldova on a firm footing, with all the necessary and appropriate procedures and oversight in place.

'Our primary goal is medical care, combined with appropriate humanitarian aid. Our second visit to the orphanage last November brought much sadness, but also hope. Two more children died over this last month in these very poor conditions, and many more are at risk, highlighting further the need for immediate medical care. With the permission and assistance of the Moldovan Government and the director of the orphanage, we have started the selection process to employ health care professionals to begin a full-time programme with the children.'

While the scale of the suffering clearly distressed Suzanne, her pain is accentuated still further as she recalls the story of some the children who were in her care.

'Nothing could have prepared me for what I saw. I chose Moldova, this small country sandwiched between Romania and the Ukraine, because I saw a documentary on RTÉ that went out late one night. Some of the scenes were very disturbing. As part of our studies we have to go abroad twice in our training to get experience. The sights we saw there would have been seen in Ireland decades ago. The children were lying on mattresses, drenched in their own urine, and they had no emotional support. Our main task was to work with the children. None of us will ever forget them.

'We have a certain level of health care in Ireland that we are used to. In Moldova, disabled children will not be accepted in the hospital without a carer from outside with them on a twenty-four hour basis. The system in Moldova is that you bring in your drugs and your own food.

'We had one child, Elviera, who had a problem with an abscess in her teeth that hadn't been stitched up properly, and after eighteen months of recurring infections she basically had a hole in the side of her face that hadn't actually healed. Every time she smiled the wound re-opened and she would bleed.

'In fact, the only disability she had was that she was an epileptic. Of course, in Ireland we no longer consider this a serious disability, but they still do in Moldova and she couldn't be accepted in the hospital. We insisted that she be taken into the hospital so we decided to set up a rota for one of us to be with her around the clock. Within twenty-four hours of her operation she was lying on a mattress soaked in blood products and urine. I stayed with her for twenty-four hours and what I saw then disturbed me greatly. She received no care from the nurses because she was disabled and she was only seen once by her doctor. She was put in a sideroom infested by cockroaches, and I spent the entire night brushing cockroaches off a child just out of surgery and, in fact, I couldn't get them off her quick enough. Any time we tried to give her fluid the cockroaches would get into the bottle and we had to throw it away and start again from scratch. This was a place where there's twelve hours electricity per day in the hospital. Thank God she wasn't dependent on any machines to keep her alive. There are no toilet facilities after 6 p.m. If the carer needed to go to the toilet she had to go outside.

'We had another child, again an epileptic, who was in a state of continual seizure and as a result she went into a coma. They refused to accept her in the hospital because she was disabled.

'One of the stories that really had a big effect on me was that of Olia. She had a congenital heart condition. What happened to her was that she was never given the proper cardiac care, she didn't get the medication she needed. On 21st of October last she lost her battle and died, aged twenty-four years. The only luxury she had ever asked for her in her life was to be baptised, but they couldn't even organise that for her. As a result, she did not get a proper funeral and is now buried in an unmarked grave on the outskirts of the cemetery where she'll never be remembered. Her little sister, who is twenty-two, was also in the orphanage. To this day, she has never received any counselling about her sister's death. She was removed one day from the orphanage and that was it.'

Suzanne and her colleagues have devised a number of imaginative strategies to raise awareness and get practical assistance for these orphans, for example, a project whereby transition year students organise a can appeal, collecting cans of non-perishable food items.

Her experiences in Moldova have caused Suzanne to become more aware of the injustices in Ireland. While thankfully there have been great advances in recent years in many areas of Irish life, not all the changes have been to our advantage. The 'Ireland of the thousand welcomes' is dead and hastily buried in a pauper's grave. Indeed Suzanne feels that our Traveller community might well have grounds to ask if it was ever anything but a figment of our imagination. Given the apartheid, Irish style, that they have been subjected to, they must find the phrase 'fellow citizens' nothing more than a bad joke.

Suzanne believes that the biggest blight on Irish society is our treatment of refugees and that the xenophobia that has emerged in recent years is nothing less than a national scandal. Listening to the many phone-ins that dominate our airwaves, it is evident that the attitude of many people towards ethnic minorities worsens on a daily basis. For all our talk of equal rights, a significant minority of people living in Ireland have not significantly improved their lot or achieved legal, economic or cultural parity. The economic, political and cultural disadvantages suffered by these Celtic outcasts are serious violations of justice.

Suzanne believes that if we are to respond adequately to the challenge to build an inclusive society we must communally face up to awkward questions: are we prepared as a society to confront the skeletons in the cupboards of the Celtic tiger? Have we a vision of our nation and its needs in the new millenium?

Suzanne is keenly aware that she needs help if she is ever to see her dreams for the children in Moldova realised.

'We are looking for support to bring the bare necessities to these beautiful children. We particularly need part-time and full-time volunteers. The greatest gift anyone could give these children is the gift of their time. We know there are many calls on people's generosity. But a little goes a long way in a country as poor as Moldova. These children are our European neighbours. They have no families, no love, no voice and no rights. They need someone to speak up for them, they need people to look out for them rather than look away, they need our concern. We invite people to join us, to be their voice and give them back their childhood and give them something to look forward to - LIFE.'

If you would like further information, or would like to make a donation or serve as a volunteer, contact OutReach Moldova at: PO Box, 8039, Dún Laoghaire, Co. Dublin.

THE MITCHELL PRINCIPLES

Jim Mitchell

Responsibility looms over Jim Mitchell like the proverbial sword of Damocles, yet it hardly seems to bother him. However, a fierce resolution to live and serve is boldly stamped on his face. An inner force exhorts him to perform his duty without any encouragement from the outside world. To understand Jim Mitchell it is necessary to journey with him on a tapestry of memories back to his childhood.

'Well, as a young person I was brought up to believe in God and we had the rosary daily without exception. Of course, every day of Lent we had Mass in the morning at 7 a.m. and my father would have the breakfast ready for us when we got back. We were also taught to be non-judgemental of others and to respect other people's points of view. So from an early age, and to this day, God and prayer have been important parts of my life. I believe in constant prayer, on the way to work or school. When should we pray? In all dangerous temptations and afflictions.

'I'm a practising Catholic, but I'm also a practising sinner and my mother, in particular, had the attitude that if you had to repent for your sins, the best way to do it was by going to the church. I go to the church every week as a means of repentance, but more importantly as a way of keeping in touch with God.'

Religion was not just for Sundays in the Mitchell household.

'Apart from prayer it was driven in to us to be honest. My mother's favourite saying was, "Honesty is the best policy". Another big thing was your word of honour. She would always urge us to keep our word.

'My father died when I was eleven. He was an extraordinarily charitable man, to a very unwise extent. He gave away lots to charitable cases when we had very little to spare. On one occasion our electricity was cut off for two reasons: he had developed a bit of a drinking problem at that stage and because he was giving money away to people with problems. For instance, on one occasion, he brought home a Traveller woman and her seven children and my mother, who was already stretched to the limit to feed her own family, had to try and accommodate them. They were given food that night and a bath and given our beds to sleep in. We had to sleep on the floor. The next day they were sent off with food parcels. Of course, my mother then had no idea how she was going to put food on the table for the next week.

'My father used to do the "Spot the ball" competition in one of the English newspapers. He won the competition and shortly after he got a cheque for seven pounds, which was a lot of money back then. My father always said he could see the profile of the Traveller woman on the cheque. Overwhelmingly, there was a huge message from my parents that you should give.

'This kind of spirit was very prominent in the area where I grew up in Inchicore. The tone was set by the Oblate Fathers, the Christian Brothers and the Sisters of Mercy in the schools. There were a lot of practical initiatives to help the poor – with the penny dinners and so on.'

To this day Jim Mitchell's faith is rock solid.

'I have absolutely no doubts about my beliefs. I never have to question them in any way, though I am tolerant of other people's views.'

He joined the Guinness computer staff in the early seventies, but he was about to scale greater heights with unaccustomed alacrity.

Having been elected to Dublin Corporation in 1974, he was elected Lord Mayor of Dublin in 1976, though still in his twenties. The following year he was elected to the Dáil for the first time, in the Dublin West constituency, and was immediately appointed to the Fine Gael front bench as spokesman on Labour. When Garret Fitzgerald was first elected Taoiseach in 1981, Mitchell was appointed to the demanding task of Minister for Justice. Since then, he has been at the top of the political tree. In February 2000 that seemed to matter very little.

'I discovered that I had a very serious illness. I was feeling fine, absolutely full of energy. One Sunday afternoon I got a pain in my tummy and it became acute. I had to be taken into the hospital in an ambulance. After a few very bad hours it went away. I resumed the next day with perfect health. Seven months later it came back again. I went to hospital, but after queuing for hours in the Emergency room I got attention and again I made a quick recovery. It came back a third time eight months later, and this time things got more serious. They operated and they found these cancerous tumours in my intestinal tracts.'

Cancer is the most feared word in the English language and Mitchell had particular reasons to be fearful.

'My father died of cancer at the age of fifty-four. My sister died of cancer at the age of forty-three. My brother died two years later at the age of forty-nine. Those two members of the family had the exact same colour hair as me and the exact same kind of face colouring whereas the rest of the family had black hair and the same colour skin as my brother Gay. I remember when my brother died; I thought to myself that there must be a very high chance of it happening to me and of course it did.'

No patient is an island. It was also a hugely distressing time for all of his family.

'I've always been lucky, and I was then, because I got a rare form of cancer from which it is possible to die, and many people do, but you have maybe a fifty per cent chance of surviving. Some people can live thirty or forty years with it.

'On the eve of the DIRT enquiry I learned that I had secondaries on my liver, which was quite a shock. The problem was that every second test came up with a contradictory message but I got the definite diagnosis in February of 2000. Not only did I have it, I had it on both sides of my liver, and not only that but I had a very rare sub-form of it, which was why it was so difficult for them to diagnose it. That was quite a moment.'

He experienced an initial sense of powerlessness because he felt that he had no control over the disease or its treatment. Yet his faith did not plumb the depth of his despair.

'I really believe that my faith and my upbringing stood to me because I believe that we just pass through this life and go on to an even better eternal life. After five minutes of shock I brushed myself down and resolved just to get on with it.'

The transplant went incredibly well. In those moments, those breaths of time, when sadness and joy share the narrow path of life hope glowed like a light in darkness. Gladness filled his heart and mind.

'I feel fine. I want to go on working. My faith has sustained me, through the bad times. Although I am a practising Catholic I firmly believe in the separation of Church and State. I would like to see women more involved in the Church and indeed in politics. I would like to see women cardinals. I really want to pass on my faith to my children the way my parents passed it on to me. I want them to believe in God even if they can't accept all of the Church's teachings. I want them to be honest and keep their word.'

GONE BUT NOT FORGOTTEN

Michael Cleary

It must have been the ultimate test of a vocation. In 1955 Michael Cleary was in line for a place on the Dublin team to play Kerry in the All-Ireland football final in 1955. The problem was that he was also attending the diocesan seminary in Clonliffe at the time. Under College regulations there was no way he would be freed to play the match. It was a straightforward choice: which was more important to him, to play in the final or to become a priest? He chose to become a man of the cloth.

Fr Mick subsequently played for Dublin under the name of Mick Casey, because of a curious rule that forbade clerical students and priests to play competitive football. A change of name was an Irish clerical solution to an Irish clerical problem. Most bishops turned a blind eye to the practice even though they knew full well what was going on.

I met Fr Mick for the last time in November 1993. In truth, I didn't recognise him. I was shocked by the deterioration in his condition. Cancer and chemotherapy had ravaged the healthy looking man that I had known for seven years to an emaciated ghost of his former self. He joked: 'Everybody tells me I look better without the hair.' I lied through my teeth and agreed with this verdict.

So desperate was I to talk about anything other than cancer that I brought up the subject of the series of articles on Bishop Eamonn

Casey that were running at the time in the *Sunday Tribune*. I knew as soon as I said it that I had made a grave error. He was very troubled about the idea of raking up old wounds and stressed, with raw passion, the hurt that journalists can cause to innocent people by malicious gossip. He added, curiously: 'Believe me, I know what it's like.' I knew there was something going on that was much more personal than just a reaction to the Casey story, but it was only a fortnight after his death, when the spotlight was turned on him with allegations that he too had fathered a son, that I understood what he meant.

Then, as I frantically searched for some way of changing the subject to another, Fr Mick reverted to type with a characteristic story: 'Have you heard the one about Casey going to confession?'

'No.'

'Casey went to Cardinal Sin for confession in New York. When he got into the confessional he began by saying: "Bless me Sin for I have fathered!"'

He laughed heartily and was back to his old self, talking with gusto about the Dublin-Kerry clashes of the 1970s. He then moved on to discuss more serious issues and posed the question: what will our children be ashamed of when they look back in forty years to the state of Irish society today?

He answered his own question by saying that God created people because he wanted someone to speak with. This was why his Word had to be made flesh. This insight reminds us that us that God is a living God, someone who loves people and loves to be loved by people. He quoted the old Celtic prayer that God is to be found with people, not in places of stone:

> Pilgrim, take care your journey's not in vain
> A hazard without profit, without gain,
> The King you seek you'll find in Rome, 'tis true,
> But only if He travels on the way with you.

The baby Jesus came as, 'the way, the truth and the life'. He came to bring 'the good news to the poor.' It was a particular kind of good news because its truth hurts as much as it liberates. Sadly, there are many cosy corners that need to be challenged and many aspects of Irish society that stand in need of liberation.

Jesus formulated an alternative model of society. This Christ – exalted even on the Cross – healed the broken, fed the multitudes, and significantly removed social stigmas, such as leprosy, and reintegrated outcasts like prostitutes and tax-collectors into society.

Fr Mick explained that Christians respond best to the invitation of Jesus to love, not by building memorials to the dead, but by giving food to the living. The secret of life is that only in love for the living is the spirit praised forever. Our challenge in the new millenium is to allow this love to be a lamp for our steps and a light for our eyes. This will call for a Christianity that has a vital, personal quality rather than being something worn ostentatiously, like a religious emblem, and for a spirituality that is deep, mysterious and beautiful, a religion that gives sympathy to our hearts and understanding to our minds.

Despite the great economic success some enjoy, the gulf between rich and poor continues to widen.

'In the Bible the question of where and how we can serve the Lord has a clear answer. We find Him in the hungry, the thirsty, the stranger and the naked, we see Him wherever people are in need and cry out for help. The Christian God revealed to us in the bruised and broken body of the suffering Jesus, continues to reveal himself wherever human suffering is to be found. From the beginning Christians were people who recognised God in the course of their daily care to others.

'In the Gospel, we find Jesus repeating over and over again the simple advice "Watch and pray". This was not merely a readiness for unexpected death. It is far wider than that. It is to be alert to the call of God in our immediate situation. All of us share the gospel call: "Seek ye first the kingdom of God".'

He reminded me that the Irish description of a disabled person as God's own person (*duine le Dia*) is a good illustration of that point. Old life, injured life, disabled life: every life is God's own life, God's special gift and task.

Someone had sent him on the motto of the Sue Ryder Foundation and he quoted it with feeling:

> For the cause that lacks assistance,
> For the wrong that needs resistance,
> For the future in the distance,
> And the good that I can do.

As we parted he responded to the uncertainty and unreality in my voice as I wished him well: 'I've a lot of fighting in me yet, but if God calls I'm ready. Life is just a long courtship with God and death is the final union.'

Six weeks later he was dead.

THE NUN AND THE POET

Sr Pauline Fitzwalter

In her late seventies, Sr Pauline Fitzwalter is still a human dynamo, though her hearing is not what it once was. To visit her home, using the term loosely, is an experience; it is like a cross between a railway station and a refuge for the bewildered. Yet despite the constant flow of callers there is a magical atmosphere about her apparently idiosyncratic community. In this frugal household love is all around.

Irish blood flows in her veins. She grew up in an Australian town called Donnybrook. Her mother was the daughter of Patrick Joseph Murphy, who came from Galway, and Catherine Sarsfield, from an island on Lake Corrib. Her childhood, though, was anything but blissful:

'My parents separated when I was three. My mother was pregnant when they split up. She was a great provider, but I don't think she fully understood the importance of displaying affection to us. My father was an alcoholic. I have known what it was like to live in a dysfunctional family and I think this has given me a greater empathy for the people I work with today.'

After she finished school she decided to become a teacher, or in Australian parlance a 'school mam'. Then a friend asked her would she present a programme on radio and she went on to concentrate on women's and children's items. Around about this time, she became engaged to be married. During her engagement, she came to realise that, although her boyfriend loved her totally, she did not love him in the same way. She broke off the engagement and threw herself into her work with such ferocity that physically, mentally and emotionally she was on the point of collapse:

'I was twenty-three at the time. I started feeling terrible pain behind my eyes. I got a panic attack and I knew my heart was at least murmuring, if I was not having an actual heart attack. I saw my face in the sideboard and it had gone purple. I wasn't afraid of dying but there was this question inside me: "What have I done for others?" I knew I hadn't done much to hurt them, but also I know that I hadn't done much to help them.

'My mother called for the priest first and then the doctor. That was her way, the eternal values were more important. The priest's name was Bertie Bree, from Dublin. He didn't anoint me because you had to be literally on the verge of death before you were anointed at the time. Then the doctor came. It was not the first time he had visited me. When I was three I had convulsions and the same doctor had visited me and said I wouldn't make it through the night; I pulled through both times.

'Looking back now, I don't think of it as a breakdown, but as a breakthrough. As I made my recovery that question inside me: "What have I done for others?" kept coming back to me. I knew my life would have to take a different route.'

After much soul-searching she decided she would follow the path of her younger sister Bernice and become a Good Samaritan sister. In 1948, when she was twenty-five years of age, she entered their novitiate in Sydney. After her spiritual formation was completed and her education was extended she returned to teaching. She subsequently became a lecturer in the novitiate. The whole course of her life was changed by a chance meeting in 1965.

'I was asked to be one of four usherettes who were to be responsible for directing the guests to their places at a ceremony in our convent, where seventeen of our young sisters were taking the veil. As the ceremony started, the Mother Superior asked me to wait outside the gate and direct any latecomers to their places, which meant that I would miss the proceedings. At the time I believed that blind obedience gave glory to God – I don't any more – and waited outside.

'After a while a man came to the gate and I said to him: "Good morning. Which sister are you looking for?" He replied: "No sister in particular, but could you help me? I'm looking for peace. The name of your convent is Mount St Benedict and the Benedictine motto is *pax*." I knew immediately that he was an educated man and then he went on to say: "I've just escaped from a mental home." He looked very rational and had a book of Gerard Manley Hopkins' poetry in his hand. He asked me if I liked Hopkins. He met me as a friend and I liked him immediately because there was a gentleness about him. He told me his name was Francis Webb. I had read a poem in the newspaper two weeks previously by a man called Francis Webb that had made a deep impression on me and he was one of the biggest names in Australian poetry at the time. I asked him if he was a poet but he said he was just a versifier.

'We had a rule in our congregation at the time which stated that whenever we had a lengthy conversation with any one we had to bring God into it. Looking back, it was a very artificial notion but I raised the God question with him. He said: "Sister, I have lost everything people consider important, but I have retained the two most important things in life – my faith in Christ and in the Church."

'He went on to tell me that he had no place to go and what he really wanted at that stage was to get a lift to a St Vincent de Paul hostel some miles away. I was struck by how such a talented man had such a modest wish. I resolved there and then I would get him a lift. I remembered that there was a young priest who hadn't bothered to attend the ceremony and who was sitting in the shade. He had said to me: "I'm sick of the sight of convent chapels." He seemed to be the obvious choice to take Francis to the hostel, so I brought the poet over to him. I was shocked at the priest's arrogance. He dismissively told Francis to thumb a lift with the lorry drivers. It was like a bucket of water had been thrown over my face because I had led Francis to believe he would get help, but all he got was rejection.

'As I watched Francis walk down the drive, I had an inner vision of Christ, that's all I can say. I knew for certain I was sending away Christ. Francis had asked for a crumb but it had been snatched away from him. I fought hard to control my temper. I had a lengthy conversation with the priest. I said to him that that man was Francis Webb. He said: "You mean the poet? He was no more Francis Webb than you are." We then went on to talk about the needy and he said there were no needy people any more. He knew that I was unhappy with his treatment of Francis and provoked me into saying: "I don't know about you Father but the Gospel is still relevant to my life." I knew I had struck a blow below the belt and I repented for my sin afterwards.

'A short time afterwards I spoke about the incident in detail to the Mother Superior. She could see that I had been deeply affected by the whole episode and suggested that we try to contact Francis. We went through the phone book and eventually we tracked down one of his relatives. Then the full story of Francis emerged. His mother died when he was a young boy and his father couldn't cope with the shock and was unable to care for Francis and his three sisters. They were brought up by their grandparents, but really had a life of emotional deprivation. The relative was able to tell me the name of the psychiatric institution Frank was staying in.

'I wrote to him and asked him to pardon me, and the priest who had humiliated him. When he got that letter he wrote straight back to me. He told me that he was in a straitjacket at the time, and to know that another person was thinking of him in that way was like a miracle for him. We began to correspond and gradually I began to see the need for a new apostolate to people who would be considered 'down-and-outs' and had no one to love them. I resolved to do something about it. Francis asked me to keep the first place in this new caring community for him. Sadly Francis died on 23 November 1973, before I had started anything. Our Lord then started to work harder on me and in 1977 I asked to be released from my congregation.

'I moved to the inner city of Sydney in 1977 and set up a new community for those who had no one to love them. Initially, I was living with just three men, which was very unusual at the time. In the first year we established a network of three houses for all kinds of victims of abuse and neglect. Over the years our community houses have mushroomed around Sydney and we look after all kinds of people, ranging from children of five to men and women of eighty. Our primary objective is to give people a sense that they are worthwhile, cared for and – most importantly – that they are loved. In the face of each of these people I see Christ. They have given me new horizons of hope in my life.'